THE SIGNAL CALLERS

SIPE * JAWORSKI
FERGUSON * BARTKOWSKI

THE SIGNAL CALLERS

SIPE ★ JAWORSKI ★ FERGUSON ★ BARTKOWSKI ★

BY BILL GUTMAN

tempo
books

GROSSET & DUNLAP
A Filmways Company
Publishers • New York

Acknowledgments

The author would like to thank the following people for providing background material and information helpful in the preparation of this book: Joe Browne and Susan McCann of the National Football League; Greg Gulas, Sports Information Director at Youngstown State University; Bruce Herman, Sports Information Director of San Diego State University; Rick Schaeffer, SID at the University of Arkansas; and the Sports Information Department at the University of California. Also, Budd Thalman of the Buffalo Bills, Charlie Dayton of the Atlanta Falcons, Jim Gallagher of the Philadelphia Eagles, and Nate Wallack of the Cleveland Browns.

CONTENTS

Brian Sipe.. 1

Ron Jaworski... 49

Joe Ferguson... 95

Steve Bartkowski...141

Brian Sipe

Once upon a time there was a quarterback drafted on the thirteenth round of the annual college draft by a very successful and prestigious professional football team. The quarterback was considered too small and fragile for the rigors of the pro game, and it was said that he didn't have a strong throwing arm. The owner of this football team referred to the selection of the quarterback as:

". . . a meaningless choice, a stab in the dark."

As for the quarterback, he admitted that he "wasn't banking on a career in professional football."

Then just why did the Cleveland Browns make Brian Sipe the 330th collegian picked in the 1972 draft. Team owner Art Modell explains:

"All I can tell you is that Brian was far down the line on our rating board. It was obvious, too, that none of the other teams had him any higher. Why they didn't, I don't know. Maybe it was his physical characteristics. He's not exactly your typical 6–3, 200-lb. quarterback, and if you stand him next to guys like Terry Bradshaw and Bert Jones, he suffers by comparison.

"I guess the reason we picked him was because we were more impressed by his coming from San Diego State, where they played a pro-style offense. In fact, that was probably Brian's most important credential, that he came out of San Diego State and had been coached by Don Coryell."

And if he wasn't banking on a career in professional football, just why did Brian decide to report to the Cleveland Brown training camp in the summer of 1973 instead of going to Law School or pursuing another avenue of employment.

"I saw an opportunity to make the squad," Brian explains, "but probably more than anything else I wanted to come to Cleveland as an experience. I hadn't seen that part of the country and I wanted to find out a little about professional football. I certainly never pictured myself as a starting quarterback in the NFL."

By listening to all these explanations, it seems that the logical ending for the story is simple. Either the quarterback was given a pat on the back and told, "Nice try, kid," or he was put on the taxi squad and phased out a year later, or maybe spent a year or two on the bench, mopped up in a couple of games, and then packed it in. Then he returned home to pursue that other avenue of employment and spent his spare time telling friends what it was like in the National Football League.

Well, obviously, it didn't happen the way. In fact, it turned out to be just the opposite, but unlike other fairy tales, it didn't happen overnight with the wave of a magic wand or the bite of an apple. It took years of patience and hard work, self-belief, and the confidence of others. It was a slow progression, a learning experience, a blend of physical and mental talents, qualities of leadership, courage, and toughness.

As it turned out, Brian Sipe had all these qualities, and he has used them, along with the tools around him, his coaches and teammates, to become one of the very best quarterbacks in the entire NFL. And a more unlikely superstar isn't to be found. Now the fairy tales about

Brian Sipe have a decidedly different ring. As one sportswriter puts it:

"Telling Brian Sipe there is two minutes to go in a game is like Popeye grabbing a can of spinach, Captain Marvel saying 'Shazaam' or giving Frankenstein a couple of electric charges behind the ears."

Ficticious characters are still used when referring to Brian, but now they are used to indicate just what a miracle man he has become. He is the leader of the Cleveland Browns, a team that had become known in the 1979 and 1980 seasons as the "Cardiac Kids," because of their last-minute heroics and never-say-die attitude. This makes them perhaps the most dangerous team in the league when they are within striking distance of the lead as the clock ticks down.

And at the helm is Brian Sipe, the man around which it all revolves. He's still not big, maybe six feet or slightly taller, and weighing about 190 pounds. He's still not overly strong. His passes still wobble and flutter, and the crowds don't ooh and aah when he uncorks them. But he gets the job done. And Brian himself says:

"The thing that separates quarterbacks is not the arm. It's intuition and instinct, which can't be measured or defined. It's something you have to be blessed with and something you have to stay aware of. As for my arm, I feel as if I can get the ball anywhere on the field at the right time, and that's all that counts."

Or as owner Art Modell says, when reminded of how low Brian was drafted:

"Nobody could see into Brian's head and heart."

The irony of it all is that had Brian come out of college some five years later, he might not have even been drafted. In 1977, the league stopped drafting after 12 rounds, and owner Modell feels Brian may have gone in another direction.

"I've often wondered what would have happened if we hadn't drafted Brian," Modell said. "He could have tried out for a team here or in Canada, but knowing Brian. I think he would have gone into another vocation."

It makes you wonder how many other Brian Sipes might be around, guys that weren't picked because of one thing or another, and if given the chance could have made it. Some, probably, but it takes a special kind of guy to start at the very bottom, and slowly and patiently make his way to the top, to stick it out when he's making a thousand dollars a game under a personal services contract for his first two years, not even a regular players' pact.

So in some ways, Brian Sipe's story is a rags to riches tale, with the prime mover in the drama being Brian himself. If he wasn't endowed with some very special qualities, none of this would have happened.

Brian Sipe was born on August 8, 1949, in San Diego, California. He was the only son of Martin and Marguerite Sipe, who also had three daughters. The family was always comfortable and Brian had a good and happy childhood.

Living in southern California and near the Pacific Ocean, Brian enjoyed the often easy and laid-back lifestyle of the area. He loved the beach and the water and when he was old enough learned how to surf, an interest that later became almost a passion. He also learned to love and respect nature and the naturally beautiful things in his surroundings.

Though he began playing sports early in life and excelled from the beginning, he didn't indulge in them in the do-or-die manner that some youngsters from small rural towns did. For many professional athletes from these small towns, sports had been a passion and way of life since they were small. They were on the playing fields and playgrounds from dawn to dusk, and often continued after dark in gymnasiums or by streetlights. They loved doing it because there is really little else interesting to do.

But in Brian's case it wasn't that way. There was the countryside itself, surfing, the beach, and many other California type activities to occupy his time. He did spend his elementary and junior high years in parochial schools and was also an altar boy at his local church. But as he got older he realized that he wanted to see all sides of life and began to shy away from organized groups.

"More than anything else," he said, "I want to be a balanced person, with everything in my life blending together."

His life in sports began early. He played his first organized football when he was in the fifth grade. By then, he was also playing baseball and basketball, and excelling in each sport. He was never especially big for his age, so he always had to use his brains and his instincts to compete on the same level with bigger, stronger boys.

He was also playing Little League baseball at that time, and in 1961, he got the thrill of a lifetime. His team went to the Little League World Series in Williamsport, Pennsylvania, and they won it all, becoming world champions, and giving Brian, who was a pitcher-outfielder, his first taste of what winning a title in sports really means.

When Brian reached Grossmont High School in La Mesa, California, he was a fine, all-around athlete and a good student. Still not big, barely six feet and maybe 170 –75 pounds, he competed successfully in all three sports —baseball, basketball, and football. And as Brian said many times before about sports: "I liked them all equally. I can't really say that one was my favorite or which one I would have chosen if I could only play one."

He was probably a little more advanced in baseball, because of his Little League experience and the fact that size didn't mean as much at that level as with the other sports. He lettered three years on the diamond, two on the gridiron and two on the hardwood of the basketball court. But while he was a good player, he wasn't one of those high school superstars who stand head-and-shoulders above the other players on the team. So the recruiters didn't come flocking around in droves. Those who came were from area schools and junior colleges from California.

Entering his senior year at Grossmont, Brian began to think about his immediate future which brought him to a rather obvious conclusion.

"Though I still liked all three sports about the same, I began to look at football as the best vehicle for me, the sport that would most likely get me into college on a scholarship."

Soon, he explored the possibilities in earnest. He spoke with representatives of a number of schools but decided to stay close to home. He would attend San Diego State University.

That, in itself, must have said something about Brian's ability then. He was, of course, a quarterback at Grossmont, and though he obviously didn't have the size or the so-called rifle arm, he must have been a good thrower, as well as a leader. The San Diego State Aztecs were a throwing football team.

Their coach was Don Coryell, currently the coach of the San Diego Chargers and formerly the St. Louis Cardinals of the NFL. Coryell has always been an offensive-minded coach whose philosophy is simple: the fastest way to move downfield is to throw the football. He practiced what he preached and ran the Aztec offense with a pro-type formation, the QB throwing from the pocket, the receivers split wide, and a variety of passing formations from which to choose.

His record spoke for itself. From the time he took over in 1961 until Brian enrolled in the fall of 1968, Coryell's Aztec teams had won 59 and lost just 11. Directly preceding Brian at quarterback were Don Horn and Dennis Shaw, both of whom went on to play in the NFL.

When Brian arrived at San Diego State, Shaw was still the incumbent signal-caller. Shaw saw most of the action in 1968 and '69, while Brian learned from the bench. In '68, Brian played with the freshman team, joining varsity as Shaw's backup the next year.

But quarterbacks weren't the only outstanding players with the Aztecs in those years. Coach Coryell attracted a bevy of fine football players as his outstanding record attests, and many of them have been or still are familiar names around the National Football League.

Coming out of San Diego before Brian arrived were the likes of wide receiver Gary Garrison, quarterback Don Horn, and running back Don Shy in 1967. The next year wide receiver Haven Moses was a number one draft choice. Fred Dryer was a top pick in 1969 as a defensive end. Shaw was a high pick in 1970 draft, and when Brian came out in 1972, teammate Willie Buchanon was a number one pick as a defensive back.

The year after Brian left, San Diego State produced wide receiver Isaac Curtis and defensive back Joe Lavender, and in 1974 came quarterback Jesse Freitas and offensive lineman Claudie Minor. A year later defensive back Monte Jackson was drafted by the Los Angeles Rams on the second round.

So while San Diego State might not be considered a real big time school, there was a constant parade of really outstanding athletes and gridiron stars, coached by Don Coryell, many of them going on to outstanding professional careers.

The 1969 season was a banner one for the Aztecs. The team was undefeated with a perfect, 11 –0, record. In 1968 they were 9–0–1, 11–0 in 1967, and 10–1 in 1966. So Coryell's teams were on a real roll. Shaw did the majority of quarterbacking for the 1969 outfit and the club was an offensive powerhouse. They won some games by huge margins, beating Cal State-Los Angeles, 49–0, San Jose State, 55–21, the University of the Pacific, 58–32, and New Mexico State by the whopping score of 70–21.

Shaw was brilliant. In the New Mexico State game, he threw the amazing total of nine touchdown passes! For the season he completed 199 of 335 passes for 3,185 yards and 39 big TD scores. He left behind some rather large shoes to fill.

But with many lopsided games during the season, Brian had numerous opportunities to get valuable game experience, and Coryell put him in whenever he could. Brian responded very well, showing a cool head under fire and the ability to move the team. In his first taste of varsity action he completed 45 of 82 passes for 557 yards and a very good completion percentage of 54.9. Coryell was sure he had made the right choice in picking his next quarterback.

The next year, 1970, Brian was at the helm and Coryell had another fine Aztec team ready to go. They were an unusual bunch. Coryell related well to his players and treated them as individuals, taking into consideration the time in which they were living and attending college.

"Don Coryell was very sensitive to the kind of guy I am," Brian says. "The whole bunch of us were a little strange, I guess. Many of the players were dropouts from other schools and other teams in the league called us the 'Renegades.'

"We'd fly down to play a team like Southern Mississippi and we'd all be wearing Levis and T-shirts, with long hair and mustaches. And when we'd get to the stadium, the other team would be wearing blazers and have neat hair, the whole thing. Just seeing us often used to infuriate opposing coaches. I guess they were afraid we'd be a bad influence on their players.

"But the thing is we always produced, and Coach Coryell knew we would, so he didn't try to change our basic lifestyles. That suited me perfectly, because while I wasn't trying to be a spectacle or anything like that, I also couldn't conform to somebody else's ideas, especially when I felt it might be injurious to my own performance.

"I've always felt that my entire life had to be in order for me to be a good football player. I can't have my concentration disturbed, and that meant at the time not having anyone hassle me about lifestyle, about my clothes, my hair, things like that. So I was always appreciative of Coach Coryell being the way he was."

On the gridiron, Brian was doing the job, and the Aztecs were on the way to another outstanding season. The offense wasn't quite as explosive as it had been the year before, but the defense improved. They won their first three games against Northern Illinois, North Texas State, and Cal State by scores of 35–3, 23–0, and 35–0. So the Aztecs weren't fooling around. For a bunch of free-spirited guys, they could play the game.

In a 31–11 victory over Brigham Young, Brian hooked up with receiver Jeff Baker on a 79-yard touchdown bomb, one of the longest scoring passes in school history. He continued to lead the club to victories, as Southern Mississippi, San Jose State, Fresno State, University of Pacific, and UC Santa Barbara all fell victim. The Santa Barbara score was 64–7, as Brian and his mates continued to hang up the yardage and the points. The team was 9–0 and looking for another unbeaten season.

Unfortunately, they came up short in their final two games. They hit a flat spot in their season and were beaten by Cal State, 27–11, and Iowa State, 28–22. But a 9–2 season was still an outstanding one as the Coryell football machine rolled along.

Brian's season was immensely successful. He completed 195 of 337 passes for 2,618 yards and a passing percentage of 57.9. He also threw for 23 touchdowns and had 20 passes intercepted. His total offense of 2,422 yards was second to Shaw's 1969 total at the time, and his passing yardage was also second to Shaw's total of a year earlier. When the season ended he learned he had been named an honorable mention All-American by the Associated Press.

One of Brian's biggest fans then and now is Don Coryell, and several years later he verbalized on the qualities that Brian began to show at San Diego State and that eventually came out even more strongly in the pros.

"It's the intangibles that make Brian so special," Coryell said, "his qualities of leadership. He's a coach's dream. He carries out instructions perfectly and his players believe in him. That's a hard combination to beat."

The 1971 season, however, turned out to be the only one in Coryell's 12-year tenure at San Diego State when the team wasn't balanced and very tough. He got caught in a transitional period, too many seniors gone and not enough underclassmen with the experience to take charge right away. And, a couple of key injuries didn't help either. It was basically a struggle all year.

That made it more difficult for Brian. Whereas he had always played from a position of command before, this season he often found himself playing catch up football. That usually meant fewer completions and more intercepts, because you've got to go long more often and the defense often knows the pass is coming.

After losing its opener, the team won four straight, then bowed to Fresno State by a 17–10 count. But the Aztecs lone score was one to remember. Brian hooked up with receiver Robert West on what turned out to be a 92-yard pass-run touchdown play, the longest in San Diego State history.

Two more losses followed, and the team found itself struggling at 4–4, a record unheard of for Coryell-coached teams. But playing under these kinds of conditions helped Brian in the long run and eventually prepared him for his career as a pro. He realizes that now.

"We didn't have that many quality players in 1971, so our philosophy was just to go out there, open it up, and try to outscore the opposition. It was a very valuable time for me, although I didn't realize it then. I think what helped me the most was to acquire a great deal of confidence in myself as a pure passer, to know that when you have to pass on every down, you can do it. In the pros it becomes a key factor, especially late in the game."

But there was also another side to Brian during that difficult 1971 season, something he will also talk about today, now that he has had time to analyze it more closely, and from a distance.

"Competing in college football wasn't the easiest thing in the world for me at the time," he says. "It wasn't really anything to do with my ability or my confidence as a player. It was other things. My mind, for instance, was filled with an awful lot of things then and

I think I was trying to put the relevancy of playing football and competing in its proper place with everything else.

"I had many questions about myself and what I would do. I guess you could say I didn't have all my values straightened out. I was quite a different person then than I am now, and at that time I didn't believe I'd make a career out of professional football. I had decided to study pre-law, but only because I had to pick a major to keep my scholarship.

"What it amounts to is that I wasn't overly ambitious then. I always felt things would take care of themselves and I just took one day at a time. To tell the truth, football was the easiest thing for me to do then, and it was also the most intriguing. In some ways, I was a product of the late Sixties, when so many divergent things were happening on the college campuses. A lot of kids were confused then about what they wanted to do."

So Brian played out the year and did it very well. The club won two of its last three games, including big wins over Arizona, 39–10, and North Texas State, 44–28, as Brian closed with a rush to end a very productive college career. In fact, he ended up to be quite a record breaker before he was through.

For the season, he had completed 196 of 369 passes for 2,532 yards, a 53.1 passing percentage, and 17 touchdowns. Though the stats were down slightly from the season before, the team circumstances dictated that. Yet he still did well enough to be declared the 1971 NCAA Collegiate passing champion on the basis of 17.8 completions per game. That's quite an honor.

He also made the Pacific Coast Athletic Association All-Star team for the second straight year, and was named an honorable mention All-American once more, this time by both the AP and UPI. In addition to that, he broke several San Diego State records, many of them held by his predecessor, Dennis Shaw.

His 436 career completions were, and still are, the most in Aztec history, as is his career yardage of 5,707. He also became, and remains, the San Diego State career leader in total offense, with 5,374 yards, surpassing Shaw who finished with 5,371. For a kid who wasn't sure of the relevancy of football, he had done all right.

By the end of the year, his attitude about the game was beginning to change somewhat, and he gives credit once again to his coach, Don Coryell.

"Coach Coryell is still one of my all-time favorite people," Brian says. "I've always admired him for far more than his coaching ability. He was able to help me put the game into proper perspective and make me see why it might be a worthwhile pursuit.

"It wasn't for the money or notoriety, at least not for me. There were a lot of lessons to be learned from football, including the challenge of trying to solve the tactical side of the game. And I really feel there are not many coaches or institutions, for that matter, who would have allowed me to progress the way I did and in the manner I did."

So Brian's career at San Diego State was over. In retrospect, it was a rather impressive, often brilliant career, but he apparently failed to make a real impression on any of the NFL scouts. If he had, he would have been picked a whole lot earlier, since quarterbacks, good ones, are always at a premium.

Of course, when draft time came around, Brian really wasn't expecting too much. He was undoubtedly keeping his options open, and couldn't have been overjoyed when he learned that some 329 collegiate football players had been picked ahead of him. But the thought of going to Cleveland and trying to make the Browns intrigued him, and with Don Coryell's encouragement, he decided to give it a try.

Despite his rather lowly selection, he had been picked by a rather successful and storied franchise, though in recent years the team's fortunes had faded a bit. The Cleveland Browns had originally been formed in 1946 as part of a new, renegade league called the All-America Conference. The AAC tried to do in the post war years what the AFL tried to do in 1960—compete against the National Football League. Besides Cleveland, there were franchises in Miami, Chicago, Buffalo, two in New York, Los Angeles, and San Francisco. So the AAC was going head to head with the NFL in several cities.

It didn't take long to see that the class of the All-America Conference was clearly the Cleveland Browns. They were 12–2 in the league's initial season, scoring 423 points to their opponents 137. And in the championship game that year they whipped the New York Yankees (yes, a football team by that name), 14–9. That first Browns team had such great football names as quarterback Otto Graham, placekicker and tackle Lou Groza, fullback Marion Motley, and receiver Dante Lavelli among others.

The team's impressive record that first year proved no fluke. Coached by the venerable Paul Brown, the Browns were 12–1–1 the next year, winning the title again, then went unbeaten at 14–0 in 1948, whipping Buffalo for their third straight AAC title, 49–0, and finally were 9–1–2 in 1949. That year they finished in a tie with Buffalo in their division, won it in a playoff, 31–21, and took their fourth straight AAC championship by beating the San Francisco 49ers, 21–7.

But by 1949, the AAC was falling on some hard times. There just weren't enough fans then to support both leagues, and as happened some 20 years later with the AFL, the All-America Conference merged with the NFL. Or, at least some of the teams were taken in to the older league in tact. Among them were the Browns, the

Baltimore Colts (formed in 1947), and the 49ers.

Of course, the established National Football League teams scoffed at the newcomers. Sure, the Browns were the scourge of the AAC, but how would they do against real football teams? Well, Graham, Motley and company showed them. They ripped through the NFL in 1950 the same way they tore apart the AAC. Losing only to the New York Giants twice, the Browns finished 10–2 to win the Eastern Division. And in their first NFL title game they whipped the Los Angeles Rams to win it all. The Cleveland Browns legend had begun.

From 1950 to 1955, the Browns were in the NFL championship game six straight years, winning three of them. They were back again in 1957. By that time they had acquired a fullback from Syracuse named Jim Brown, still acknowledged by most today as the greatest running back of all-time. They were still a winning team in the late '50s and early '60s, though not as dominant as they had been.

But in 1964, they did it again, winning their division and whipping Baltimore, 27–0, for still another National Football League crown. They were back again the following year, though they lost to Vince Lombardi's Green Bay Packers.

Even when some of the older stars retired, the Browns replaced them with other fine players, such as quarterback Frank Ryan, running back Leroy Kelly, and receiver Paul Warfield. The Browns remained a winning franchise into the late 60s. The Super Bowl began in 1966, but while the team made the NFL and later the AFC playoffs in '67, '68, '69, and '71, they never could get to the big one. But they had been a good club in 1971, finishing 9–5 for the year, and when Brian Sipe reported to his first professional training camp in the summer of 1972, the team expected to be solid once again.

Brian felt he was coming in with some good credentials. Besides being the 1971 NCAA passing champion, he had played very well in two post-season All-Star games, the East-West Game and the American Bowl Classic. Still, there was a question about his size. The trend for the previous years had been toward bigger, taller quarterbacks. The theory was that with the linemen getting bigger, the quarterback had to be at least 6–2 or 6–3 to see his receivers over the onrushing linemen. But Brian wasn't satisfied with that reasoning.

"All you had to do was look around the league and judge a few of the top quarterbacks on their performances. You found a lot of them were either my height or shorter."

This was true. Perhaps the most notable "short" quarterback was Fran Tarkenton, who set a multitude of passing records before his retirement. But it was said that Fran could get away with it because he moved out of the pocket so often. Yet a look at the past quarterbacks showed that many of the greats, such as John Unitas and Sonny Jurgensen were not really any taller than Brian.

Prior to Brian's arrival, the Browns quarterback for a number of seasons was Bill Nelsen, a fine signal-caller and passer. Yet, he was prone to injury and played on two bad knees and a lot of guts. In 1970, the club had drafted a highly-touted All-American from Purdue, Mike Phipps, and after backing up Nelsen for two years, club officials were hoping Phipps could do the job. Nelsen agreed to stay on as a backup in case the youngster faltered.

"Bill was really banged up," recalls Brian, "and he probably should have retired a few seasons earlier. But he had a lot of courage and loyalty and agreed to play again in 1972." Head coach Nick Skorich and his staff didn't want to carry three quarterbacks. Yet Brian had shown enough ability that they didn't want to cut him outright. So they put him on the taxi squad for the year.

This meant he was a part of the team . . . but then again he wasn't. He sat in on all team meetings and was there when the quarterbacks met. He also practiced with the team, but he couldn't play in the games. On Sundays, he was on the sidelines in street clothes, wearing a headset and relaying information and advice from the coaches who were sitting in the press box.

The taxi squad rules were set up a little differently in those days. For one thing, to get a player onto the taxi squad he first had to be waived through the league which meant another team could pick him up if they wanted him. But no one claimed Brian. So he was unwanted by all the other clubs in the NFL. Secondly, a player on the taxi squad didn't have a regular players' contract. So Brian was retained on a personal services contract by the Cleveland Browns for $1,000 a game. Today, that type of taxi squad does not exist.

At any rate, though he was practicing with the team, Brian was not making a great impression. He himself admitted that he "really bombed out." And owner Art Modell, in looking back, recalls there were some very serious questions about Brian.

"We realized Brian had ability, but we didn't know if he wanted to play, or for that matter, if he could. So we taxied him because we just weren't sure."

Phipps had a fairly good season in a first-string role, and the rest of the team was still strong. They finished the year with a 10–4 mark and made the playoffs, where they were promptly eliminated by the Miami Dolphins.

Brian went home in the off-season uncertain about continuing his career and not knowing where it would go. He still didn't truly feel a part of the team. Upon hearing that Bill Nelsen was finally retiring, his spirits got a boost. He figured he'd be the backup to Phipps in '73 and might finally get a chance to play. But shortly afterward, he heard that the club had made a trade to get veteran Don Horn, who had also gone to San Diego State a few years before Brian.

"That shows you the kind of impression I made," Brian says now. "They felt they had to make a trade for a backup quarterback."

That wasn't all. When the 1973 draft rolled around, the club tried to fill some immediate needs by taking wide receiver Steve Holden, then running back Greg Pruitt, who would become a full-fledged superstar. Then on the fourth round they picked a quarterback, Randy Mattingly of Evansville. This is what really shook Brian Sipe.

"When they drafted Mattingly I knew my spot on the taxi squad wasn't even safe," Brian recalls. "That's when I realized for the first time that I wanted a spot on the club. And that's when I really applied myself for the first time. I went through a complete attitude change and finally took my profession seriously. I'll say this much for the coach, Nick Skorich. He must have seen my ability and believed in me during that time I was goofing off. He's the guy who stuck with me, and I can't say I really helped him much."

That's quite an admission for a professional athlete to make. Brian came to camp and worked harder. It was Mattingly who was cut before camp broke, but it didn't help Brian too much. It just assured him a place on the taxi squad for a second straight year. More practice, more headphones, another year of $1,000 a game. But he stuck it out and was glad to be there, and waited patiently for a chance to move up the ladder.

The club itself was in a state of transition. Most of the old guard were gone or just about gone, and some of the young players had not yet arrived or just wouldn't arrive. The team struggled through a 7–5–2 season, and missed the playoffs. Most observers agreed that the

Browns were a team on the way down. There were just too many weak spots and not enough depth.

When Brian reported in 1974, he had finally won himself a job. At last he was the number two quarterback. No more taxi squad. After two seasons of waiting and learning, he hoped to get a shot at some real NFL action. And once he knew he had the backup job, Brian's attitude changed again. His old confidence resurfaced and he began to feel he wanted more. It's the kind of ego all the great ones have, a belief in their own ability to get the job done, and done better than anyone else.

"I'll admit that once I had the backup it occurred to me that I should be starting. I decided right then and there that if I were going to do it, if I were going to be involved in it, then it was worth doing right."

In his first two years as a starter, it had really been a matter of the team carrying Phipps, rather than he carrying the team. Mike just couldn't seem to find any real consistency and establish a workable pattern of leadership. When the team collapsed around him in 1974, things just kept getting worse, and little by little, Coach Skorich began taking a look at Brian Sipe.

The club was badly beaten in its opener that year, Cincinnati taking a 33–7 victory. They bounced back to beat Houston, 20–7, but the following week were taking another bad beating from St. Louis. That's when Brian got his first taste of NFL regular-season action. He entered the game in the final minutes, the contest already lost. He threw two passes, completed one for six yards as the game ended with the Cards on top, 29–7.

A week later the club took another beating from the Oakland Raiders. For the proud Browns and their fans, this kind of treatment was unheard of and very difficult to accept. Early in the fourth period Phipps was hit hard and feeling groggy was helped to the sidelines. Enter Brian Sipe.

On his first play from scrimmage he handed the ball to running back Hugh McKinnis, who promptly took off on a nifty, 44-yard touchdown run. Some 65,000 fans at Municipal Stadium were on their feet and cheering, and Brian liked the sound of it all.

When the Browns got the ball again, he decided to take to the air. Trailing 37–24, a couple of touchdowns could pull it out. Brian dropped back and calmly connected on a 12-yarder to Gloster Richardson for a first down. Then he went to his back, McKinnis, and completed a 10-yard toss for another first. The fans wondered if this kid from San Diego was going to pull off a miracle finish.

But the heroics ended right there. The Raiders and their "Soul Patrol" secondary were waiting for the youngster. Knowing he was going to throw they intercepted him, three times in the final eight minutes of the game, and wound up with a 40–24 triumph. Brian called it a "humiliating experience," but it was experience and he could only get better for it.

Losses to Cincinnati and Pittsburgh followed, and the once proud Browns found themselves with a 1–5 record as they prepared to host the Denver Broncos. Once again Phipps got the start, and the Browns fell behind. Brian was called into the game by Skorich in the fourth quarter with the Broncos leading 21–9.

For a backup quarterback to come during the closing moments of a losing game is an especially difficult task. And even more so for a young, inexperienced signal-caller. A veteran spending his last year or two as a backup might have more success in this situation because of the control and knowledge acquired over the years. Brian saw how quickly this could backfire in the Oakland game. But he tried to concentrate on the job that had to be done.

The first time the Browns had the ball, Brian began

moving the club, mixing the run and the pass. He completed one pass, then another, then a third. He was being cool and efficient. His fourth straight completion brought the ball to the eight yard line, and from there, he took it in himself on a bootleg play for the score. The kick made it 21–16 and the Browns were within striking distance.

Moments later, the Broncos were forced to punt and young Greg Pruitt lugged the ball back 72 yards, bringing it down close. Brian then quickly moved the club to the one-yard line, and took it over himself for his second score and for the winning margin. The kick made it 23–21, and that's the way the game ended.

His performance earned him several starts in the second half of the year, though Phipps still saw the bulk of the action. When the season ended, the Browns had a 4–10 mark, the worst record in the history of the franchise. But they had discovered one thing, Brian Sipe could play the pro game after all.

He had completed 59 of 108 passes for 603 yards and an impressive 54.6 completion percentage. He threw for just one score and was intercepted seven times, but his stats can be explained by the fact that he was often playing catch-up. In addition, he ran 16 times for 44 yards and scored four touchdowns running the ball over.

By contrast, Mike Phipps had completed 117 of 256 for the year, and that was only a 45.7 percentage. He tossed for just nine scores and had 17 intercepted. There were questions about Phipps' ability to run a ballclub successfully. He hadn't made an outstanding impression as a starter. So when the season ended and Brian left for home, he felt he had a good chance to win that starting job in 1975. And this time he really felt he was ready.

But shortly after the season ended, the Browns made a coaching change. Skorich left and was replaced by one-time all-pro lineman Forrest Gregg. Brian had a talk with the new coach shortly after he was appointed. The news wasn't welcomed, but he took it philosophically.

"Coach Gregg told me that Mike was still his number one man," Brian recalls. "I understood the situation and really didn't feel I was being slighted. I had to believe my time would come and I'd get the chance to play. The thing I had to do was make sure I was ready."

The 1975 season quickly turned into a total disaster for the Browns. The team went down early and before the smoke had cleared they lost nine games in a row. For the Cleveland Browns this was a study in total futility. Brian found himself playing even less than he had the year before. It seemed as if Gregg was going to sink or swim with Phipps and decide how far he could go with the now veteran QB.

Brian got a start in the sixth game against the Redskins. It was close for nearly three quarters. The Skins had a 9–0 lead in the third when Brian led the Browns on a 94-yard touchdown drive, ending it with a 15-yard pass to tight end Oscar Roan. It brought the score to 9–7, but the Cleveland defense wilted in the fourth and the Skins won, 23–7.

After nine losses, the team won three of its last five to finish at 3–11. But it was still a humiliating season. Phipps completed 162 of 313 passes which didn't seem bad at first glance. But he threw for just four touchdowns and had 19 passes picked off, a very negative statistic. As for Brian, he only got to throw 88 passes, fewer than the year before, and he completed 45 of them for 427 yards and one score. He had three picked off. One of the few positive things about the season was Greg Pruitt's emergence as an outstanding running back. The former Oklahoma flash gained 1,067 yards on

217 carries for an impressive 4.9 average. And with a 3–11 team, that was good!

It had to be a discouraging situation for Brian at this point. Two years on the taxi squad and now two as a backup, and still no sign of a change with the Cleveland brass. He'd be going into his fifth season, counting the cab squad, and many players would be trumpeting the old play-me-or-trade-me ploy by this time. But Brian continued to bide his time. He actually wanted to produce for the Browns.

"I'm from Southern California," he told one reporter, "and it's about as different from Cleveland as you can get. Don't get me wrong, I'm not passing judgment on either place. But I will say one thing. The fans in Cleveland are football crazy and they deserve the best football they can get. And I'll tell you, I'd break my neck giving it to them if I could."

The Browns were beginning to pick up some better players. In 1975 a trade brought them wide receiver Reggie Rucker, a proven talent. And the 1976 draft produced fullback Mike Pruitt (no relation to Greg) and wide receiver Dave Logan. These were all players who would play a major role in the team's revitalization.

But as far as Brian was concerned, the preseason of 1976 seemed to be more of the same with no changes. Phipps was playing and he wasn't. In fact, in six preseason games he threw just 20 passes. So he wasn't even getting the playing time then. But he still refused to make waves, even though he voiced concern about the situation.

"I still don't think of myself as a backup quarterback," he said. "And I won't as long as I know I can play in this league. I'm sure I have the capabilities and talent to be a regular. But not getting the playing time does concern me. I definitely feel I can play here or with anybody, but I would like to stay here with the Browns because I'm very satisfied being part of this organization."

But how long could he wait? There were still whispers that Phipps was holding the top job because he looked like a pro quarterback. He had the size. Somehow, people continued to feel that Brian might be too small, that he might not be able to withstand the pounding that goes with regular duty. But they would never really know . . . unless.

With Phipps playing and the team winning four of six preseason games there was the feeling they might be able to turn things back around fairly quickly. The opener that year was against the New York Jets, but when the Jets jumped to a quick, 10–0, lead after one period, the nearly 67,500 fans at Municipal Stadium felt it was going to be more of the same.

Then in the second period, Phipps suddenly caught fire and was playing like the quarterback everyone had thought he would be. He moved the club downfield three times with his passing and ended each drive with a touchdown toss to give the Browns a 21–10 halftime lead.

In the early minutes of the third period Phipps had them on the move again. He was mixing his plays and throwing very well, keeping the Jets defense off balance. Then he decided to try to keep them off-guard by running a bootleg play himself. It worked perfectly as Phipps sprinted for a 24-yard gain. But at the end of the journey was Jets safety Schafer Suggs, and he put a crunching tackle on the Browns' quarterback. Phipps got up slowly, his arm hanging limply by his side, and he walked off the field. It was diagnosed as a separated shoulder.

Suddenly, in the first game of the new season, and with things going so well, Brian Sipe was in the game and facing a new situation. The team had the lead and momentum. If he blew it, his teammates could lose confidence quickly . . . and so could he.

But Brian stayed cool. He continued to call the same kind of game that Phipps had, and he was executing just as well, faking smoothly and deftly, and throwing with confidence and precision. He kept the team moving, completed seven of the 10 passes he threw, two of them for touchdowns, and led the team to an impressive, 38–17 romp.

"Sipe showed why we have so much confidence in him," said receiver coach Raymond Berry, a sentiment echoed by others.

But Brian quickly showed his class. Though he probably wanted the starting job more than anything he ever wanted, he hated to get it because a teammate was hurt. Phipps would be out indefinitely. When reporters began asking Brian questions about his performance and the triumph, he said, with emphasis:

"I appreciate all the attention I'm getting, but what you should know is that Mike Phipps won this game for us. If he hadn't brought us back after being down 10–0, I might not have been able to do what I did."

But the main point was that Brian was suddenly the main man, if he stayed healthy, for perhaps the rest of the season. Coach Gregg and the rest of his staff, as well as many Cleveland fans, undoubtedly wondered if Brian could do the job. Outwardly, the coach was telling everyone he could.

"I was extremely pleased with the way Brian played. He came in and kept the offense moving without missing a beat. Backup quarterbacks always take part in all the mental work, but they don't always get that much time directing the team in practice, and they play little in games. Brian came in and showed how well prepared he was, and that was impressive.

"Both I and the team have a great deal of faith in

Brian Sipe. We feel he can win for us. He's intelligent, throws well, and has plenty of self-assurance. So we don't plan any major changes or major deals regarding the quarterback position."

Now Brian would find out what he wondered for so long. Could he do it? He had some fine players working with him. Running back Greg Pruitt was becoming a superstar, Reggie Rucker was a fine wide receiver, and in 1976, veteran Paul Warfield returned to the team. Warfield was a brilliant wide receiver who had starred for the Browns in his early years, was traded to Miami, had spent a year in the World Football League, and had now come home to finish his career in Cleveland. He provided stability for any quarterback.

Though Brian was anxious to get off to a good start, the next three weeks really tested his strength of character and ability to withstand advertity. A team cannot give up 120 points defensively in three games and expect to win.

Against mighty Pittsburgh, Brian completed 15 of 34 passes for 193 yards, but the Steelers won easily, 31–14. He had 18 completions for 134 yards against Denver, but the Browns were buried again, 44–13, in a sloppy game in which fumbles and interceptions didn't help the Cleveland cause.

Then came Cincinnati, and this time Brian was hot. Throwing much of the afternoon because his club was trailing, Brian set a Cleveland club record with 26 completions, 12 of them coming in a row at one point. He threw for 290 yards in a game, but his outstanding performance was more than off-set by defensive breakdowns and the club lost again, 45–24. So after the opening victory, they had lost three straight and seemed on the brink of going down the tubes for a third straight year.

Though Brian was well aware that the Cincy game

was his best effort with the Browns, he refused to elaborate on the positive things he had done, admitting only, "We moved the ball well," then adding quickly, "but the idea is to win."

After some defensive adjustments the team went up against Pittsburgh again. Brian was playing well and had the club on the board, but he was shaken up in the second period and had to leave the game. While being taken to the hospital for observation, the new back-up, Dave Mays, came in and helped engineer an 18–16 upset victory. It would be ironic if, after getting his chance, Brian was shelved by an injury. Suffering a slight concussion, he was ready to go the next week against Atlanta.

He played well again, completing 12 of 18 for 134 yards as the Browns won once more, 20–17. The following week against San Diego, he was really on the mark. Passing with pinpoint precision, he led the club to still another win, 21–17. And in doing so, he set another club record by completing 82.1 percent of his passes with a 23 for 28 day. His confidence booming, Brian seemed to be getting better each week.

The next week the club stumbled, losing to Cincinnati, 21–6. Then came a surprise. Mike Phipps had recovered enough to be activated and Coach Gregg decided to start him against Houston. There is kind of an unwritten law in the NFL that a starting quarterback shouldn't really lose his job because of injury. So while many of his teammates and new fans thought Brian was being jobbed, it was obvious that Phipps would have to perform extremely well very quickly to stay in there.

Phipps played a little more than three periods and was obviously not sharp. The defense was playing well and the Browns hung on to an 8–7 lead. Finally, Coach Gregg felt he had no other choice but to go back to Brian. Right away the club seemed to come to life. Brian moved them downfield and from then 10, Greg Pruitt tossed an option TD pass to Brian Duncan for the score. Minutes later Brian had them moving again, and he took care of things with a 23-yard scoring aerial to Oscar Roan. The final was 23–7 and one issue was settled once and for all. Brian Sipe was the Browns' number one quarterback.

Brian continued to play well, directing the team to victories over Philadelphia, Tampa Bay, Miami and Houston, before the club was upset on the last day, 39–14, by Kansas City. Yet the Browns had been the surprise team of the year, going from 3–11 to 9–5 in just one season. They didn't make the playoffs and there were still many areas on the team that needed strengthening, but they seemed to be coming on. And they had found themselves a new quarterback.

For the season, Brian completed 178 of 312 passes for 2,113 yards and an impressive 57.1 completion percentage. He threw for 17 touchdowns and had just 14 picked off. He had done all that was asked of him, and one of the first to say it was Mike Phipps, the man he replaced.

"Brian was the key to what the Browns have done this year," Phipps said. "I'll admit he surprised me, and I think he surprised himself, too."

Brian didn't agree. "I always felt I could run this team," he said. "But I've also matured a great deal as a quarterback and I'm very happy I had the opportunity this season to develop my skills."

So Brian went home this time as a number one quarterback on a winning team. It still wouldn't be easy to keep the Browns above .500, but it was a challenge. For one thing, they surrendered more points than scored, 287 to 267. That's a very unusual situation for a 9–5 club and was an area for concern. When Brian returned for the 1977 season, he found himself a much more sought after personality and also began revealing more of himself to the public. They quickly learned he was not your ordinary, everyday, gung-ho football player who thought about nothing else.

First he addressed himself to the continuing questions about his size, strength, and arm. After all these years, it took a great deal of patience to continue this kind of talk.

"I keep hearing those kinds of things," Brian said, "but in truth, I don't think I have any shortcomings as a quarterback. The talk about my size and my arm doesn't bother me because I know I can compensate inside myself for any physical shortcomings I might have.

"I remember one game last year when I had to roll out of the pocket to my left. There was a big defensive back after me and he had the angle to run me down. At the last instant I saw one of our receivers in the back of the end zone and I let it go. He caught it over his head on the way out of the end zone. Now I threw that ball from just the other side of the 50 and if he hadn't caught it but just let it hit the ground, I'm sure it would have traveled some 60 or 65 yards. So enough about my arm.

"You hit any secondary—I don't care how good they are—with the unexpected and chaos results. I just don't think a lot of people in Cleveland totally realize what my potential is. I'm fully capable of doing whatever has to be done to win, and that includes throwing the long ball."

Again, Brian's confidence had become unshakable. It's as if he knew what he could do once he got a little more experience and a stronger team around him. Yet he didn't come across as cocky or arrogant, and he often talked about aspects of the game that most players don't mention or perhaps don't even think about.

"There's so much about football that's mental and not physical," he told a reporter. "At San Diego State we regularly played people who outclassed us physically and we'd end up taking them apart. What we did was destroy them mentally by beating them at something they thought they couldn't be beaten at. It works."

He also talked about the great concentration he felt he had to maintain during the season. He refused to let anything shake it and said he didn't even read the newspaper stories because the input would affect his concentration.

"The less I can focus my concentration, the more trouble my body has performing its physical tasks," is the way he put it. "What I try to achieve during the season is a relaxed state of concentration. I simply try to cleanse my mind of the pressures that people are trying to heap on me. That way I perform better, and when I really think about it, maybe that's what went wrong with Mike. He just couldn't get away from the pressures."

And speaking of Phipps, the Browns ended any potential quarterback crisis for 1977 by trading their former number one choice to the Chicago Bears. So Brian was finally getting the job. At last the team had staked its future with him. And with a 9–5 season behind them, it wasn't too unrealistic to hope for a playoff spot in '77.

Both Brian and the Browns were off to a fast start in the new season. In the opener against Cincinnati, he connected on 15 of 22 passes for 198 yards and directed the offense with confidence. The defense, too, looked improved, and the Browns took a 13–3 decision.

A week later the team was in a real donnybrook with the powerful New England Patriots. The lead changed hands several times as both offenses were in high gear. Brian hit tight end Gary Parris for a 26-yard TD strike, then later connected on an eight-yarder to Greg Pruitt. At the end of regulation time, the game was tied at 27–all.

In overtime, Brian drove the Browns into New England territory. With just 4:45 gone, veteran Don Cockroft kicked a 35-yard field goal to win it.

Brian had completed 18 of 25 passes for 199 yards and two scores. More and more he was beginning to look not like just a good quarterback, but an outstanding one. Someone asked Brian if he felt less pressure with Mike Phipps gone.

"It really doesn't make any difference," he said. "I've felt for a very long time that the job was mine unless someone else could take it away. I think Mike will have a good opportunity with the Bears and I wish him well."

Brian continued to play well even though the team lost to Pittsburgh and Oakland. Victories over Houston, Buffalo, and Kansas City followed, then an upset loss to Cincinnati, 10–7. But the team was at 5–3 and if they finished strong as they did a year earlier, they still had a shot at making the playoffs.

Then came a return match with the Steelers. This time the Browns hung in there tough. Similar to the New England game, the lead changed hands, back and forth. But early in the second half, disaster struck. Brian was being chased out of the pocket by several Steelers and he was belted down by defensive tackle Ernie Holmes. Clutching his left shoulder, he left the game. Later, the news was not good. Brian had a fractured shoulder blade and would be lost for the year.

Pittsburgh went on to win the game, 35–31, and with young David Mays at the helm the rest of the way, the club managed to win just one of its remaining five games, giving them a disappointing 6–8 record for the year. In a rather unfortunate way, it showed just how valuable Brian Sipe had become.

Though the injury cut his season short, Brian continued to show enormous potential. He completed 112 of 195 passes for 1,233 yards and nine scores. His passing percentage was 57.4 and he had a long TD strike of 52-yards. The only negative stat was his 14 intercepts. But the fact remained that the team had been a winner with him, a loser without him.

With his usual candor, Brian said he didn't feel his injury was intentional, but also said that others had been and gave some unusual views on the game.

"I'm sure Holmes didn't mean to hurt me," he said. "But in the first game against them when I banged up my elbow and shoulder, the damage was done by another of their linemen and it was definitely a cheap shot. I really think the quarterback should be given more protection. One thing I would recommend is no hitting in the head. I've heard bells a few times and I remember a game last year with Kansas City when the defender had a clean shot at me but chose to hit me in the head with his forearm. There was no need for it.

"I guess you could say I'm a purist. I don't care much for the violence. I know it's part of the game, but football to me is more like a game of chess. If you take a man's knight, you shouldn't throw it against the wall. It's poetry, a concentrated kind of ballet, and it's for those moments that I play the game."

And while he still knew that his best years were ahead of him, Brian also had his own views of the game and looked forward in some ways to when it would all end.

"The last year or so I've been giving my immediate future a whole lot of thought," he said, "and I made a real commitment to football. I'm most interested in getting this team into the playoffs. But I've also finally decided that I want to get one clear shot at becoming the best in the world at my particular skill.

"So I think I'm playing the game mostly for my own inner goals. I can't complain about the financial security because it enables my family to enjoy the things my natural talents can provide. But what really turns me on is playing good football, like when my receiver and I both see a defensive back doing something and we both react simultaneously.

"Yet I can't honestly say I live my whole life just to be a good quarterback. It's part of everything, and being a good quarterback · arises out of some of my total philosophical needs. Still, I've been doing this since about the fifth grade and there are times when I look forward to being done with football. I don't really think living in a football world gives you a valid view of the real world."

So the world according to Sipe is often a lot different than it is with many other athletes. Yet with all his philosophical statements, once the season begins Brian is all football player with a concentration matched by few. Forrest Gregg had left with one game remaining in the '77 season. The new coach was Sam Rutigliano, a street-smart native of Brooklyn, New York. Rutigliano had coached at every level, from high school to the pros. He had been an assistant at Denver, New England, with the New York Jets and then New Orleans Saints before taking the head job with the Browns. He was a fighter with a great deal of experience and a man highly re-garded as a football tactician and for his ability to han-dle and motivate players. The Browns felt they now had the right man to bring the club back to the top.

The draft that year brought some more defensive help, a big tight end named Ozzie Newsome, who was thought to have tremendous potential and would add another dimension to an already potent air attack. As for Brian, he worked to get back in shape by playing a variety of off-season sports.

Coaching changes don't always bring on instant suc-cess, especially when the new coach hires new assistants and goes about putting in a new system. So in many ways, 1978 was very disappointing for the Browns. It was the first year of the 16-game schedule, and the club expected to battle Pittsburgh and Houston for the AFC Central crown.

They basically played uneven football for most of the season. The offense and defense often couldn't put it together at the same time. Opening with three victories over San Francisco, Cincinnati, and Atlanta, they were derailed in overtime by Pittsburgh. Beaten by Houston, and winning over New Orleans, they then lost to Pittsburgh for a second time. And against their divisional rivals, the Oilers and Steelers, the Browns weren't putting the points on the board. When they lost to a mediocre Kansas City team, 17–3, they were a 4–4 team for the first half of the season.

Brian came under heavy criticism once again. The fact that the Browns weren't putting many points on the board against the contenders made people wonder whether Brian was capable of producing against the best. The critics were silent when he came up big against Buffalo, 41–20, but the team reversed gears and lost to Houston, 14–10, and Denver, 19–7. The running attack, with Greg and Mike Pruitt, was solid, and the blame went to the quarterback. The team was also 5–6 which placed them out of contention, and that didn't help.

Fortunately, for Brian and the Browns, the offense suddenly seemed to find itself. They whipped Baltimore, 45–10, and tough Los Angeles, 30–19. Despite a 47–24 loss to Seattle, the offense played well, and outlasted the New York Jets, 37–34. In those four games alone, Brian threw for 1,088 yards and 10 touchdowns. A season-ending loss to Cincinnati, 48–16, didn't really count, because Brian took a shot from Ross Browner and Glenn Cameron and suffered another concussion.

Another year had ended with a disappointing 8–8 record. But in some ways there were many more positive things about it than the 9–5 season of 1976. For one thing, Brian had come on very strong. He finished by setting club record for attempts with 399 and completions with 222. That was good for 2,906 yards, a 55.6 percentage, and 21 touchdowns. Plus he had just 15 interceptions. He wound up the fourth-ranked passer in the AFC behind Terry Bradshaw, Dan Fouts, and Bob Griese, some pretty good names. The club had scored 334 points, the most since 1969. The problem was that the defense gave up 356 and that had to improve.

After the season, Brian was open with his feelings and described what he learned and why he felt the Browns and he were both going to improve.

"I still feel I'm far from reaching my potential," he said. "But that four-game streak we had at the end was very reassuring to myself and the team. If I had known before those four games what I know now, our attack could have broken open earlier, and I owe it to the coaches for sticking with me when things were tough.

"But you've got to remember that with a new coaching staff it takes time to understand your role. The coaches did a great job of getting us past that and now we have a very good understanding about what Sam and the others want. They, in turn, have become familiar with my strong and weak points.

"One thing we started doing toward the end of the year was throwing deep by design. I've always said I can throw a ball as long as necessary, but I needed coaching. I didn't have the ideas of the philosophy of getting the ball deep. You can't just have your receivers try to run past people.

"We also began putting in new plays and formations, and ran our play action stuff more. In the latter part of the season I started understanding slot throwing where I had Ozzie Newsome by himself on one side, and Reggie Rucker and Dave Logan on the other. By utilizing Ozzie's speed going deep we really burned some people, and when they got around to covering Ozzie deep, they had to leave Reggie or Dave free running out of the slot and we were able to burn some other people. It was all like a light going on upstairs. All of a sudden everything started falling into place and I was sorry we didn't have more time."

Complicated business playing pro quarterback. No one learns it in a day, or a year, or even in a few years. It takes time. The hope was now that Brian would be peaking at the same time the team did. In the off-season he worked on the weight machines for the first time, hoping to increase his strength for the long season ahead. "I'm getting older. I need to be more durable," was the way he put it.

He was also beginning to get his due in the press. One Cleveland sportswriter called him "The Indispensable Brown," adding, "The Browns have only Sipe (at quarterback), a charismatic leader who in four straight games last season looked good enough to pitch the Browns into a Super Bowl . . . No quarterback looked better."

Perhaps that was a foreshadowing. For in 1979, Brian Sipe would really come of age and earn total respect from his peers throughout the league, and he would begin to weave some of the last-minute magic that would earn the team the nickname of the "Cardiac Kids."

It started the first week against the Jets. The Browns came from behind three times as Brian pitched a pair of TD tosses to Greg Pruitt and Newsome. They still trailed, 25–22, with just 30 seconds left, when Brian took them 66 yards to set up a Cockroft field goal that sent the game into overtime. A pass interception with just 24 seconds left in OT enabled Cockroft to boot a 27-yarder for the game-winner, 28–25.

A week later Brian passed the club into a 20–0 lead over the Chiefs only to see K.C. come back to take a 24

–20 advantage with just 3:19 left in the game. But again the Browns came back. Brian directed a nifty 74-yard drive, using the clock beautifully, and he passed to Reggie Rucker from 21 yards out for the winning score with just 52 seconds remaining. The final was 27–24.

The next week the Colts took a 10–0 lead, but a Cockroft field goal and 35-yard TD pass from Brian to Dave Logan drew the Browns even. Then late in the fourth period Brian went deep again, connecting on a 74-yarder to Newsome that set up Cockroft's winning field goal with just 1:51 left. The 13–10 victory gave the team three last minutes victories in three games. And Brian Sipe was playing beautifully.

"Improvisation was the key to winning this game," Brian said. "I was grab-bagging. With all the plans you make, you have to be able to react when the defenses have them figured. We won the first three games because we have guys with the talent to adjust. I'll tell you something, if we're close near the end of the game, the fans better not leave."

When the Browns soundly beat the Dallas Cowboys, 26–7, for their fourth straight victory, it began to look as if the team was finally playoff-bound. Brian continued his great play with touchdown passes of 23 yards to Dave Logan and 52 yards to Ozzie Newsome. The win was tempered, however, by knee injuries to defensive end Lyle Alzado and running back Greg Pruitt, two very key people.

Their absence didn't help the next week as Houston stopped the Cleveland express, 31–10, and the next week in a wild game, Pittsburgh broke the Cleveland defense down and won, 51–35. Even with the loss, however, Brian tied a Browns record with five touchdown passes and had a career high of 351 yards passing.

Though the team had slipped to 4–2, Brian Sipe was in the midst of a fantastic season. After six games he had completed 107 of 209 passes for 1,575 yards and 13 touchdowns. And with Greg Pruitt out, he had become the focal point of the Cleveland attack.

Brian was to perform brilliantly all year long, but the team faltered in key spots. Alzado never regained his early-season form though he returned. Greg Pruitt tried to come back, but was hurt again and needed surgery. When the club whipped the Eagles, 24–19, on November 4, they were at 7–3 and still in the playoff picture.

In that game, Brian did it again, driving his team to two touchdowns in the final four minutes, the final one coming after a 71-yard drive which Brian directed in just five plays. Now Brian Sipe was getting accolades from all over.

"Almost nobody on this team is indispensable," said veteran running back Calvin Hill, who was finishing his career in Cleveland after some brilliant years at Dallas. "Any of us can go out and somebody else can come in. But not Brian. He's playing so well that we feel we can score anytime we get the ball, anytime we need to score. Today we hurt ourselves several times, but Brian brought us back."

As for Brian, he was finding everything almost hard to believe. "I'm not going to try to analyze what's happening or what it all means," he said. "I'm just going to enjoy it, and try to keep doing it. The greatest thing about this team is that we're never out of a game, no matter what. It's the intangibles that make this team different. This team has character."

But key injuries continued to mount. Defensive tackle Jerry Sherk, one of the best in the league, was lost for the year with a staph infection in his leg. The team lost to the Seahawks, then beat the Dolphins mainly because Brian passed for a career high 358 yards. A tough, 33–30, loss to the Steelers (Brian got 333 yards in this one) was followed by a 14–7 victory over Houston. So the team was 9–5 with two games left.

Brian's performance against the Steelers was especially significant, because he played so well just days after learning his father had died of a brain tumor in California. Brian asked that the information be kept confidential until after the game so it wouldn't be over-dramatized. But after the game, Coach Rutigliano couldn't restrain himself from talking about his quarterback.

"Right now, Brian has to be the most productive quarterback in the NFL," the coach said. "I wouldn't trade him for any quarterback in the league, including Staubach or Bradshaw. Brian is just a fantastic young man and he does something every day to prove it. Because of his productivity, we are going into the 14th week of the season and we're still in the race, even though we all know we have to do some growing up as a team."

After the Browns had beaten Houston, Oilers linebacker Greg Bingham also had high praise for the rival quarterback.

"He's one of football's great quarterbacks now, no doubt about it," said Bingham. "If Brian was in Pittsburgh, the Steelers wouldn't miss a step. He's a real inspiration because he's a guy who stayed with it and kept getting better. And he's done it without a real great throwing arm. It goes to show you that a quarterback can be successful without a great gun."

A damaging, 19–14, loss to the Raiders in the fifteenth game really hurt the Browns' chances for the playoffs. They would now have to win the finale with Cincinnati to have a shot at a wildcard berth. The game was close all the way. Brian passed them to a 6–0 lead with a 33-yarder to Dave Logan. But Cincy capitalized on Cleveland mistakes to take a 13–6 lead. A Mike Pruitt touchdown closed it to 13–12 early in the fourth period.

Cincy then got a field goal to make it 16–12. Had the Browns not missed both extra points, a field goal would have won it for them. But Brian had to go for the TD. He had the team moving and they were on the four-yard-line with one play left. Dropping back, he threw for the end zone. The ball went off the fingers of Ricky Feacher and the game was over. Cleveland had lost, finished at 9–7, and missed the playoffs.

"It was a frustrating year in a lot of ways," Brian said, afterward, "because we had so many games like today, where we could have won but didn't. But looking at the other side of it, we had the character to come back and win the close ones. I thought we'd make it today because we had made the big play so often this year. 'One more time' I said to myself as we broke the huddle. But I was forced out of the pocket a little and had to throw sooner than I want to, but I still felt it would be caught.

"As for myself, I know there is still plenty of room for improvement. Any quarterback who retires and even at that time believes he has all the answers is either a fool or ignorant. I am still learning and I expect that's the way it will always be.

"I see this team as much better next season and for years to come. The surface has just been scratched and I see us going forward as a group. I'm a bit older than many of these players, but quarterbacks usually have more longevity and I believe we still have a lot of time together."

It would be difficult for anyone to complain about Brian's season. He had completed 286 of 535 passes for 3,793 yards and 28 touchdowns. His passing percentage was 53.1 and he threw 26 intercepts. He also ran the ball 45 times for 178 yards, the most of his career. His passing yardage was second in the NFL to Dan Fouts and he tied Steve Grogan of New England for the most TD passes.

"Brian is what we call a 'gamer,' " said quarterback coach Jim Shofner, "and I can't think of any higher praise. He's a guy who is at his best when the adrenalin is flowing, when he's under the pressure of a game. His strongest asset is running a football game, taking the week's work and applying it, which a lot of quarterbacks are unable to do. He's got the intelligence to analyze situations and act accordingly."

It was no secret that Brian was really appreciated now. In July of 1980, he signed a new four-year contract estimated to be worth about $1.25 million, and that would make him the highest paid player in Browns' history.

"I'm ecstatic, really thrilled," Brian said. "The new contract puts me at level comparable to other NFL quarterbacks in terms of similar experience and production."

There were also some honors beginning to roll in. He was an all-pro now, and after the season he learned that *Sports Illustrated* magazine had named him the NFL's Most Valuable Player.

Still, he remained a very private person, living with his wife and daughter (now there are two) in the small seaside town of Encinitas, California. He often declines to do interviews, doesn't do endorsements or take speaking engagements. His feeling seems to be if you can't accept them all, which you can't, than it isn't fair to accept any.

Because he often finds himself replaying lost games over and over in his head, he needs his private time at home with his family in the off-season. It's important for him to unwind and get his head together again.

"I want to keep my private life private," he says.

"And living here is just perfect for me. It's just re-markable the way they absorb people here and treat ev-eryone the same. No one is a celebrity."

A new season began and the Browns looked very strong. The top draft choice was the Heisman Trophy-winning halfback from USC, Charles White. Greg Pruitt was coming off knee surgery and would be used more as a pass receiver out of the backfield. But Mike Pruitt had taken up the slack by becoming a 1,000-yard runner himself in 1979. The offense looked to be more potent than ever, and the defense improved as well.

Strangely enough, in the preseason Brian looked ter-rible. His timing was off and there were rumors of a sore arm. Brian denied it by saying his arm was always some-what sore at that time of year. Whenever the team had a terrible preseason, the critics were always ready with an attack. By now, Brian was too much of a professional to let it bother him, but he wondered when it would stop.

It didn't help when the team came out flat in its open-ing game and got blasted by the New England Patriots, 34–17. The Browns were never in the game even though Brian completed 22 of 35 passes for two scores and didn't throw any intercepts. But one local sportswriter said Brian's stats were "misleading," adding you couldn't blame it all on the defense. "Sipe and Company are just as much to blame for this humiliating opener of a new decade for this proud franchise," the man wrote.

Then when the club lost to Houston, 16–7, in a Mon-day night game the following week, they came under heavy fire once more. What happened to that explosive offense? It had all but disappeared. Even when they beat Kansas City the following Sunday, 20–13, the club did not look particularly impressive. Rookie Charles White was the offensive star, running for 59 yards and catching seven passes for 100 more. Brian was 23 of 36 for 295 yards and seemed to be finally loosening up.

"I told you my arm was not sore," Brian told reporters, afterward. "I never even hinted that it was. I think the problem was that we played the first two games as if we were looking forward to the playoffs already instead of doing what we had to do then and there."

The next week was a barnburner with Tampa Bay. And when Brian failed to complete his first six passes, heads turned. But after that he was almost perfect, hitting on 22 of his next 26 for 318 yards and two touchdowns. He set a club record by completing 13 in a row at one point and became the first quarterback to throw for more than 300 yards against the Tampa Bay defense. The Browns won it, 34–27.

But there still wasn't consistency. Denver beat the Browns, 19–16, as Brian had 20 of 40 for 258 yards, not a good day by his standards. But an easy 27–3 victory over Seattle, followed by a 26–21 defeat of Green Bay put the team back on the track and got them ready for a big one with Pittsburgh. The only problem was that Brian sprained a knee and didn't know if he could go.

Yet at game time he was there. But it was Pittsburgh that got the lead with 10 points in the first period. That's when Brian decided to scrap the game plan. "They have a superior running defense," Brian said, "but as far as I was concerned, they were vulnerable to the pass."

So Brian began throwing and he put on quite a show, completing a club record 28 passes in 46 attempts for 349 yards and two scores. And he had to do it the hard way, rallying the team for two scores in the final period to pull out a 27–26 victory. The Cardiac Kids were back.

"Brian was just remarkable," Dave Logan said, after catching eight passes for 131 yards. "Before the game was over, we used every pass pattern in our book, every one, and they all worked."

The next week Chicago fell, 27–21, as the Browns won

their fourth straight, and the week after they whipped Baltimore, 28–27. In the Bear game Brian was 23 of 39 for 298 yards and that gave him a career total of 13,534 yards, moving him past both Frank Ryan and Otto Graham, and making him the Browns' all-time leading passer. Though records mean little to him, he said this one was a real thrill.

Against the Colts he was pinpoint accurate, completing 22 of 29 for 212 yards. The Browns were now at 7–3 and tied with Houston for first place in the AFC Central. As for Brian, he was completing 60.3 percent of his passes and had thrown for 2,671 yards, more than anyone except Dan Fouts of San Diego. And he was the top-ranked passer in the AFC.

A 16–13 loss to Pittsburgh followed, but then the club won three more, whipping Cincinnati, Houston in a big one, and the New York Jets. In the Jets game, Brian broke his own club record for completions with 30 of 41 for another 340 yards. He was in the midst of an incredible season, and the Browns were 10–4 and a game ahead of the Oilers.

The next week against the Vikings they became victims of some of their own magic. The Browns were leading the game 23–21, but the Vikings had the ball in their own territory with time for just one play. Quarterback Tommy Kramer threw the old Hail Mary pass, putting the ball far downfield to the goal line as three receivers and four defenders went for it. The ball was batted into the air and was plucked out by Ahmad Rashad, who backpedaled into the end zone for a miracle touchdown. The Vikings had won.

It was a significant victory or defeat, because it left the Browns at 10–5. Now they had to beat the Bengals in the final game to win the division. Losing would mean not making the playoffs at all if the New England Patriots and San Diego Chargers won their games. It was a complex system, to go from division champ to also-ran with one game. So it was the biggest game in years.

And it was an incredibly hard-fought game from start to finish. Tied at the half, 10–10, and 24–24 after three, both clubs battled into the final session. With time running out, Brian drove the Browns into Cincy territory, and Don Cockroft booted a 22-yard field goal with 1:25 left to win it, 27–24. The Browns had done it, finishing at 11–5, and winning the Central Division championship.

Afterward, there were compliments all around. Coach Rutigliano couldn't say enough about Brian, who was 24 for 44 for 308 yards in the final game.

"Brian is probably the Most Valuable Player in the league," said the coach, "only because he took a fairly good team, with very average coaching, to the division championship."

Sipe was quick to return the compliment. "Sam allowed me to play the game of football I play best," he said, "and turned my career around. I think he deserves the credit for making this win possible. He allowed us to concentrate by keeping things loose. We came into a must-win situation with a lot of young players and we could easily have choked."

Brian had completed one of the greatest seasons a quarterback had ever had. He completed 337 of 554 passes for 4,132 yards for a 60.8 completions percentage. His 30 touchdown passes were a team record and he had just 14 intercepted. He was the top-ranked passer in the entire league and had thrown for the second greatest number of yards in league history, beaten only by the 4,715 yards thrown by Fouts. He also had the lowest percentage of interceptions in the league.

So Brian Sipe had come full cycle. He was an all-pro, and named NFL Most Valuable Player in several polls. He was now universally known as one of the two or three best quarterbacks in football, and many people feel he is currently *the* best. But there was no time to rest on laurels. The playoffs were in the offing.

The Browns would go up against the Oakland Raiders, winners of the wild card game over Houston. The Browns were considered favorites because the game would be played at Municipal Stadium. It was a scoreless first period, as the players were having problems on a frozen field with a wind-chill factor of minus 37 degrees. The wind was blowing hard, making it difficult to keep hands warm, and Brian was having a tough day.

The Browns got on the board first in the second period when cornerback Ron Bolton intercepted a Jim Plunkett pass and returned it 42 yards for the score. But veteran Don Cockroft missed the extra point, so it was 6–0. Oakland went ahead before the half on a Mark van Eeghen run and an extra point. In the third period the Browns got a pair of Cockroft field goals for a 12–7 lead.

At the outset of the final session, the Raiders drove 81 yards in 11 plays, van Eeghen scoring again, giving them a 14–12 lead. But the Browns didn't give up and began a final drive in the last minute. They marched from their own 15 to the Oakland 14 for a first down with just 56 seconds to play.

On first down Mike Pruitt plunged for a yard to the 13. Everyone figured they'd run twice more, then bring Cockroft in for a relatively easy field goal to win it. But instead on the second down, Coach Rutigliano sent in a pass play.

"I thought the run was logical," said Brian. "But they wanted that pass play. They thought we'd score, and so did I."

Brian took the snap and dropped back. He looked for Dave Logan, the primary receiver, but saw free safety Burgess Owens coming up to double cover. So he looked for tight end Newsome cutting across the middle of the end zone. He threw toward him, but the ball fluttered in the wind, giving strong safety Mike Davis an opportunity for an interception.

It was a shattering blow. The Raiders ran out the clock to win the game. Afterward, there was a lot of second-guessing in the Cleveland locker room. Rutigliano defended his decision, claiming a field goal was no cinch at the windy open end of the stadium.

"I just figured that Brian would probably throw the ball into Lake Erie if no one was open," the coach said, "but competitor that he is, he went for the touchdown. Look, one play doesn't win or lose a game, anyway."

Despite a 13 for 40 day with three intercepts, Brian wouldn't make excuses.

"I'm not singing the blues," he said. "We did things in dramatic fashion all year. It's only fitting that we lose in dramatic fashion."

Kicker Cockroft was not happy. "Before the final play I looked at Sam and smiled," he said. "He smiled back. He knew I was ready. I think Sam knows I could have made that kick. But it's his job to decide, not mine."

Oakland's all-pro cornerback, Lester Hayes, agreed with Cockroft and put it in no uncertain terms. "They had the game locked up if only they had used Cockroft's toe," said Hayes. "But they tried to score. It just wasn't logical and it cost them a season."

Yes, it was a terribly disappointing finish. And winning it all is the goal of every player and coach. But in other ways it was a terribly good season. The team has finally turned the corner and should be back for another crack next year and for seasons to come.

But, all in all, it was an incredible season for Brian Sipe. So it ended on a disappointing note, this was perhaps the first time people hadn't criticized him. There are no more doubts, no one will ever again question his size or his arm, or his ability. Nor will they claim he doesn't look like a quarterback.

Not bad for a 13th round draft choice, a guy who came to camp in 1972 just to see Cleveland and check out the pro football scene for a year or two. A lot of players have come and gone since then, but Brian Sipe is still there, working to become the very best at his position. He certainly has arrived. Oh, yes, he certainly has.

Ron Jaworski

When Ron Jaworski was drafted by the Los Angeles Rams out of Youngstown State in 1973, the nickname he received from his teammates was almost predictable. Because of Ron's very powerful throwing arm and his Polish ancestry, he was quickly tabbed "The Polish Rifle."

That suited Ron fine, no problem. The problem was that Ron was having difficulty cracking the L.A. lineup, where a game of musical quarterbacks had been going on for a number of years. Before long, he was speaking out about his situation, saying things that management and even some teammates and fans resented. Soon, fewer and fewer people were calling him "The Polish Rifle." Not that the name wasn't applicable anymore. It's just that it was supplanted by a new nickname—"Jaws."

At first glance, Jaws must have seemed a simple play on Ron's last name. No. Jaws alluded to the noises that came out when Ron spoke. The mouth didn't stop. The jaws moved and the words came. Ron should be playing, Ron should be starting, if Ron got a chance he'd throw his way into the Hall of Fame, play me or trade me, I can do a better job than the other guys.

Ron's constant chatter and incessant griping finally got to a lot of people in L.A. Still, the Rams wanted to keep him and offered him a long-term contract. But he had had enough. Jaws said he'd rather play out his option and he literally forced the Rams to deal him. That's when he arrived in Philadelphia, the City of Brotherly Love. . . and a losing football team. The Eagles had been down so long they didn't know where up was anymore.

It didn't take Ron long to get the jaws working. Though he had been in the league four seasons, he had never been a starting quarterback and had thrown just 124 passes in his entire NFL tenure. Yet he went in as a leader, as the man who *was* going to be the Eagles quarterback now and for a long time to come. And he took some of the veteran Eagles by surprise.

Tackle Stan Walters remembers: "Ron was totally unlike any quarterback I had ever been around," he said. "I had played with Ken Anderson in Cincinnati and he was very precise, very businesslike. And when I came to the Eagles I played with Roman Gabriel and Mike Boryla. They were both loners and had that quarterback mystique about them.

"Then Ron comes along and I did a doubletake. He was so cocky, so loose. He started cracking jokes on the practice field and cutting up in the lockerroom. I really began to wonder, 'Can this crazy guy play quarterback in the National Football League?' "

But Ron had a method to his madness. Though he was coming into a new situation, the kind of situation where the new man usually eases himself in, wins respect slowly by his attitude and his actions, Ron saw it differently.

"When I first came to Philadelphia," he recalls, "I found a bunch of guys shell-shocked from losing. They had been through some very lean years and they just didn't know what it was like to have fun anymore, to enjoy the game. They were quiet and kept to themselves and I said right away, 'Hey, this has got to change.'

"So I went around patting guys on the back, telling them everything was gonna be cool. I went out and drank beer with them. At first they weren't sure where I was coming from, but I guess I just slowly wore them down. I might have been a little different, but I was real."

That entire incident says a lot about Ron Jaworski. He didn't go to Philadelphia and perform magic. He had to learn and grow with the team. He worked long and hard with head coach Dick Vermeil to improve his skills, control his game, and to perform within a tight, team concept. Ron improved as the entire team came on, and by 1978 they were contenders. Two years later Vermeil, Jaworski and the rest made good their promise to the long-suffering fans of Philadelphia. The Eagles were in the Super Bowl!

Even with all that success, though, the basic Ron Jaworski hasn't changed. He still has the arm that warrants the title of Polish Rifle, and he still sounds off when he thinks something has to be said. In fact, to the nickname of Jaws, his friends have added still another—"Dial-a-Quote."

Ron's story is not a typical one. He always did things a little differently, but wasn't afraid of hard work and had a set goal in mind. And when the goal was football, that meant playing, not sitting the bench.

"I just love the game," Ron has said. "And I mean it when I say I would play for nothing. If I wasn't in the NFL I could easily see myself working all week in a factory and playing in a semi-pro league on weekends. The game itself is fun and there's just nothing like the feeling you have after a win."

His outspoken comments notwithstanding, Ron Jaworski's road to the Eagles and to his present, lofty status, was not an easy one. He was born March 23,

1951, in Lackawanna, New York, which is a suburb of Buffalo. Ron was the youngest of three children (he has a brother and sister) and his parents were of Polish ancestry. In fact, Ron remembers as a child whenever there was a serious family discussion, his parents would speak to each other in Polish, instead of English.

Lackawanna, New York, was what is known as a steel town. The huge Bethlehem Steel plant was the principal source of employment for many people there. Steel towns are usually filled with pretty tough men, blue collar workers, who work, drink and play hard. Sports are always an important part of town life, and many prominent athletes have come from the steel country. Joe Namath and basketball's Pete Maravich are just two products of the Pennsylvania steel towns. There are others.

It wasn't long before young Ron was playing on the streets and sandlots, and while he was always a very thin kid for his age, he had the toughness and was willing to compete with anyone. Football began in earnest when he was about thirteen attending the McKinley Elementary School. Neighborhood games were often crude and rough, but they were a lot of fun. In fact, Ron still recalls what he remembers was the first big game of his life.

"We used to play what we called the Turkey Bowl game every Thanksgiving morning," he says. "It was a neighborhood game and one year we were really all excited about it. To us then, it was The Game, and you couldn't find one that was more important.

"We didn't even have uniforms or anything like that. We'd just choose up sides. Some kids might have a helmet or some other scattered piece of equipment, like pads, but most of us just played in our street clothes. There was always one kid who would show up wearing a big pair of combat boots. But we wouldn't let him play unless he changed because no one wanted to have to tackle those boots."

By the time Ron reached Lackawanna High School he was a fine all-round athlete, playing baseball and basketball, as well as football. In fact, for a while, baseball was his favorite and there was a time that both the St. Louis Cardinals and Pittsburgh Pirates organizations were taking a long look at him and talked about signing him when he graduated high school. Tall and thin then, Ron was nevertheless a catcher, principally because he was one of the few boys who had the arm to cut down baserunners.

"My arm was very strong, even then," Ron says. "I remember I used to throw from a crouch position with all arm. I didn't even have to get up and get my body into the throw to cut down runners. I always had great velocity on the ball."

While in high school, Ron met a girl named Liz Pasherb, who would later become his wife. She was a cheerleader, a year younger than he and they met when she helped Ron up after he took a bad tumble out of bounds during a game. Naturally, Liz Jaworski remembers those days quite well.

"Ron and I started dating in high school, but not steadily," she says. "There are people who think he's thin now, well, they should have seen him then, all skin and bones. In fact, I never thought of him as the football hero-type. I knew he played all three sports, but it wasn't until the second time that we dated that I learned he was a quarterback.

"But I hardly ever got to see him then. It was unbelievable. He was always playing some kind of sport. And in the summer it was almost 24 hours a day. The only time I knew I'd get to see him for sure was after a game."

Actually, Ron wasn't always a quarterback. When he

entered Lackawanna High as a freshman he was a running back and a wide receiver. But that soon changed. There is a simple explanation as to why. As Ron says, he became a quarterback when "somebody noticed I could throw the hell out of the ball."

From the first, Ron played an all-out, go for broke kind of game. He had a positive, optimistic approach that dictated that he could always make the big play.

"I've always been a positive person, a positive thinker," he said. "I don't have time for negative people, people who are always copping out, making excuses, and complaining they can't do this or that. They're whipped before they start. I believe everything begins with a positive idea. Positive thinking is the key to success in business, education, pro football, anything you mention."

That philosophy was helped by both Ron's baseball and football coaches at Lackawanna. They contributed to his attitude and to the type of game he played when he graduated.

"The baseball coach was a great believer in positive thinking," Ron says. "He wasn't much for the percentage moves like sacrifice bunts and squeeze plays. His attitude was rather why settle for one run when you can score three or four? And he'd always say to me, 'OK, Ron, pick out a good pitch and knock it out of the park.'

"The football coach was pretty much the same way. His philosophy was, 'Don't tell me how big the other guy is, just go out there and knock him on his butt.' So I learned early that the mind is our most powerful muscle. If you think you're tired, you'll feel tired. If you feel like King Kong, you'll tear people up. That's me. I go out there thinking I'm gonna complete every pass."

He certainly completed plenty of them in high school. By the time he was a senior he was just about at his full height, a shade over 6'-2", but he still weighed barely 160 pounds. Yet he was a high school superstar, and as a senior he was given the Kelly Award, given annually to the best all-round athlete in northern New York State. Liz Jaworski says that it is still one of Ron's most treasured trophies.

But it was also getting down to decision time. During his senior year, the 1968 season, he was throwing long whistling passes all over the field and beginning to attract a great deal of attention. The scouts and recruiters began coming around in earnest. Both Boston University and Boston College wanted him. So did Syracuse and Georgia Tech. And he was getting serious feelers from a number of Big Ten schools, including Ohio State.

However, his first reaction toward college was a negative one. He just didn't want to go. In fact, he began giving serious consideration to the baseball offers he was getting from the Cardinals and Pirates.

"It was a case of just not wanting to go to college," Ron recalls. "Maybe it was because there were no real role models in my immediate surroundings. Both my older brother and sister didn't go to college and I just didn't see why I had to."

He remembers his parents getting into some long discussions about the situation. They knew that life in a steel town was very difficult and really short on a future. They were determined that their youngest son take advantage of his athletic talents and use the scholarship offers to go to college. But there were some other considerations as well.

"I know some of the offers I had were real good ones," Ron says, "but although I didn't know for sure, I felt that at 6'-2", 160 pounds I was a real bean pole and a big-time operation would just burn me up. I didn't know if I could go to a place like Georgia Tech and compete with all those big studs.

"And there was still something else. I knew my main talent was my ability to throw the ball. What if I did go to a place like Ohio State? Even if I won the quarterback job I'd be spending most of my time handing the ball off. I felt that kind of situation wasn't conducive to improving the talent I had."

Then there was the offer from Youngstown State University. What's that, where's that? Most football people would have a similar reaction. Youngstown what? It was a small school in Ohio that played in the Mid-Continent Conference and was an NCAA Division II school, not exactly big time. The Youngstown Penguins went up against the likes of Central Michigan, Tennessee Tech, Akron, Gustavus Adolphus, Xavier, North Dakota State, and similar schools that don't appear on national television or go to the Rose Bowl on New Year's Day.

The coach there in 1969 was Dwight "Dike" Beede, who had been the head man since the football program started in 1938. Needless to say, Youngstown State didn't attract the usual high caliber of player, and even there were a number of fine performers. There weren't enough to generally create a really solid team. Plus the school was in a bad period, having gone 4-5 in 1967 and 3-6 in '68. Yet there were reasons that Ron found himself attracted to the school.

When Coach Beede and his quarterback coach, Jack Klebe, visited Ron they told him they would be running an offense similar to the pros. They said that as quarterback, he would get the chance to throw the ball some 30-35 times a game.

"That's what really excited me," Ron says. "I was already envisioning a pro career, but I knew I'd never make it if I went somewhere where I had to run the ball and get all beat up. When they promised me the chance to throw the ball like that I felt I would really have a chance to develop the talent I already felt I had."

So in the fall of 1969, Ron surprised the big-time recruiters by packing off to Youngstown for a career that many thought would leave him hidden in anonymity for the rest of his football days. Let's face it, if a pro scout heard there was a guy named Ron Jaworski playing down at Youngstown State, and running an offensive formation called the Side-saddle-T, he wouldn't exactly be lining up to buy his plane or bus ticket.

Actually, the Side-saddle T wasn't as strange as it sounds. It was very similar to a pro-set, but had some slight variations. Ron never really objected to it, and wouldn't have remained quiet if the formation was not suited to his passing prowess.

"It was actually a very old formation," Ron explained. "In some ways it was a variation of the single-wing, but it was done with a pro set. In other words, there were two running backs, a pair of wide receivers, and a tight end. The difference was that the quarterback didn't line up directly over the center. It was the coach's belief that if you lined up under the center, the opposition knew where the ball was going on every play, right to the quarterback. Why give them that if you didn't have to.

"So what I'd do was have my right foot pulled back, putting me slightly to the side of the center, and I'd take the ball almost as if it was a short pass back. That way, there was also the option of snapping the ball directly back to the halfback or fullback, and in that way it was like the single-wing. When we did that, the back getting the ball would roll one way and I'd roll the other. And since everyone is usually keying on the quarterback, then everyone will be drawn my way and that frees the guy with the ball going the other way until the defense reacts.

"It was an excellent offense for us because we really played a lot of teams who had better personnel and we

needed that kind of offense with that kind of deception
to more or less put us on a par with those teams. What
we didn't have in ability, we made up for in trickery."

That was true. Ron saw considerable action as a
freshman, but the Penguins only won a pair of games
and finished at 2-6. They even played two or three fewer
games than the big-time schools. And their offense
scored just 132 points while the defense yielded 243.

The next season was even worse. The club hit rock
bottom and had a forgettable, 0-9, season. It must have
been terribly frustrating for a guy like Ron who always
has a burning desire to win. He was the number one
quarterback by then, and losing week after week must
have made him think he would have been better off
elsewhere. But he stayed cool and passed for 1,411
yards. He was getting an education.

There was some improvement the next year as the
team came back to 2-6. Most of it was in the defense,
however. Without much talent around him, Ron's offense put just 101 points up and his passing stats failed
to match his sophomore season. At this point, the odds
of any NFL team drafting him must have been very
long.

But in 1972, Ron's senior year, the team finally managed to put some players around him, and for the first
time he got a chance to really open up the Penguin offense, and put to use all the things he had learned the
past three seasons. The team actually lost its first three
games before it all began coming together.

Then, against Northern Michigan, Ron cranked up
and tossed for four touchdowns to spark a 37-36 victory,
the club's first win of the year. After that, the Penguins
whipped Akron, Xavier by a 47-7 count, Central State,
tied with Central Michigan, and then lost its final game
to Indiana of Pennsylvania. But a 4-4-1 record was the

best since 1966 and Ron Jaworski's strong arm and fine passing had attracted a number of professional scouts.

He had completed 139 of 259 passes in 1972, good for a school record 2,123 yards and 18 touchdowns. That was good for a 53.7 passing percentage. His career stats read 325 completions in 658 attempts for 4,612 yards, a 49.4 percentage, and 32 touchdowns. Despite the lack of top-flight competition, collegiate notoriety, and an outstanding team, Ron never uttered a moment's complaint or regret about attending Youngstown State. He had made his choice and then had gone about making the most of the situation, as was his style. Now, he would have to wait for the 1973 pro draft to see if any NFL teams thought as much of his ability as he himself did.

"I always knew I had the ability," Ron said, without really bragging. "What I didn't have was the big-time exposure. And I don't suppose many people felt a player out of Youngstown State could be drafted on a high round."

But when the draft rolled around, a lot of people were shocked. Ron Jaworski was a second round pick of the Los Angeles Rams and the 37th player in the entire country chosen by a pro team. He was also the third quarterback taken, behind Bert Jones, who would become a superstar and was labeled at the time as a "can't miss," and Gary Huff, who never really made it big. He was chosen ahead of Joe Ferguson of Arkansas, who would become a star with the Buffalo Bills and who had been an All-American.

"I thought it was a real honor to be chosen that high," Ron said, "but I was really shocked when I learned the Rams had picked me. They were not on the list of teams I thought might be interested. I was aware that they had just acquired John Hadl and Roman Gabriel was still there then. So that gave them two fine veteran quarterbacks and I had figured there was no way they'd use a high pick on the quarterback with guys like that already there."

The Rams, of course, had been a highly successful NFL franchise. They joined the NFL in 1946 and by 1949 were playing for the championship. They were in the title game four straight years, winning once, and they remained a solid team for years. After some slow years in the early and mid-'60s, they rebuilt and by 1967 had an 11-1-2 record. Afterwards, they remained formidable, though never winning a world's title.

There was something else about the Rams that seemed to often exist within the team. That is, there was always fine talent at the quarterbacking position, and always a problem for the coaches in deciding who was number one. In the early 1950s the team was led by the talented Bob Waterfield. Then, along came the equally good Norm Van Brocklin, and the two players vied for the number one position for a number of years.

After Waterfield retired, Billy Wade came along, and he challenged Van Brocklin for the starting job until the Dutchman was traded to Philadelphia, where he led the Eagles to a title in 1960. Then in the early '60s, the Rams drafted a big, strong-armed quarterback out of North Carolina State, Roman Gabriel. It was thought Gabe would be the answer for years.

But just as Gabe was developing into a first rate pro, he was hurt and a rookie named Bill Munson stepped in and did an outstanding job. For the next several years it became a guessing game whether Gabriel or Munson would be getting the playing time. It usually went to whomever was healthiest at the time. Finally Munson went, and Gabriel settled in with the back-up, a black quarterback named James Harris from Grambling.

Then, before the 1973 draft, the Rams surprised everyone by acquiring Hadl from the San Diego Chargers.

A few weeks later they drafted Ron. So there were three established signal-callers on the roster before Ron even went to camp. No wonder he was surprised by his selection.

Suddenly, there were two. In a surprise move, the Rams sent Gabriel to the Philadelphia Eagles, the same team they had sent Van Brocklin to years before. The big guy was apparently having problems with Carroll Rosenbloom, the L.A. owner, and wanted out. That's why the team picked up John Hadl.

So Ron came into camp thinking he might have a chance to make the team after all. He was excited about his first pro camp, but there was one thing that saddened him.

"My Dad wouldn't be able to see me play ball as a pro," he said. "He died in 1971 when I was a junior at Youngstown. I remember when I was a freshman and still not playing much, he would drive for hours from Buffalo just to see me run on the field and hold for the point after. He was my biggest fan."

There was someone else who made an impression on Ron before he began a pro. "Joe Namath had come into Buffalo with the Jets in 1972 to play against the Bills. I came up and bought a ticket from a scalper just to get in to see him. I remember just studying him as he warmed up and I analyzed everything he did and compared his moves to mine. I thought he was the greatest and I still do."

Being confident and a positive thinker, Ron wanted to strut his stuff in a hurry. He wasn't going to come into camp and act like a frightened rookie. He didn't think a quarterback could act that way and still get the respect of the players around him. The Rams had a new head coach in 1973, Chuck Knox, and Ron wanted to impress him, also.

But perhaps the man he impressed most was Dick

Vermeil, who was the quarterback coach of the team in 1973. Vermeil would move to UCLA the following year, then resurface as head man in Philadelphia in 1976. So his future and Ron's would be closely intertwined in the coming years. But in 1973 Vermeil remembers how the brash rookie from Youngstown took charge of the offense immediately during practice sessions and scrimmages.

"Ron would get in the huddle and take charge," Vermeil recalls. "There were some outstanding veteran players there, but Ron let them know that he was the quarterback and the boss. That's something you can't coach. I liked his native intensity. He was a competitor and guys like that always find ways to win football games."

The problem in 1973 was that the Rams decided to go with just two quarterbacks. Before the regular season began, Ron was placed on the taxi squad. That meant he practiced with the team, went to all the meetings, but couldn't dress for the games. It's not an easy situation for a player, especially an intense competitor such as Ron. That's when he began trumpeting about his own abilities. Whenever a reporter or someone would ask Ron about his feelings regarding the taxi squad, he would tell them he knew he could play in the NFL and if given the chance he'd pass the Rams into the Super Bowl and himself into the Hall of Fame. Some of the stories got blown out of proportion, but he soon began getting the reputation of a player who didn't mind running off at the mouth.

But even though he was taxied for the entire year, one very good thing did come out of it, and that was Ron's association with John Hadl. The veteran signal-caller was coming to the end of an outstanding career, most of it spent with the San Diego Chargers in the AFL before the two leagues merged. In fact, Hadl was known as the first home-grown AFL quarterback, since when the league began play most of the signal-callers were ex-NFLers who found a way to play a few years longer.

At any rate, Hadl liked Ron and his strong desire to play and contribute. He kind of took the youngster under his wing and his tutelage proved invaluable to Ron.

"John helped me both on and off the field," Ron says. "He helped me form my overall approach to the game, to life in pro ball as a quarterback. We lived across the street from each other in Marina Del Rey and drove back and forth to practice together. Sometimes we'd stop for a few beers and do a lot of hanging around together."

Hadl taught the youngster many of the little extra things that might ordinarily take a rookie a number of years and a number of hard lessons to learn. He suggested, for instance, that Ron always be friendly with and generous to his offensive linemen. If they like and respect you they'll give it just a little bit more and take additional pride in protecting you, Hadl pointed out.

"John was very wise about it. He left the coaching to the coaches, and they can certainly be of great help in as far as looking at films and giving you the game plan. But John more or less tutored me in the real points that you can only get by having game experience. And, of course, I wasn't getting any of that in 1973."

With Hadl at the helm, the Rams compiled an impressive 12-2 record to take the NFC Western Division championship. Unfortunately, they were beaten by the Dallas Cowboys in the playoffs, 27-16. Ron went home, hoping for the real shot the next year. In the off-season, he and Liz were married and they returned to L.A. in 1974 full of optimism, though neither one particularly liked the Los Angeles lifestyle.

It was the same cast of characters. Hadl was one of

the top-ranked QB's in the league in '73 and it was assumed he would be starting. Harris, though he had thrown just 11 passes as the back-up the previous season, was still highly-rated. So Ron knew he had an uphill climb, and he continued to tell people he knew he could do the job.

In the first preseason game that year against the Cleveland Browns, Coach Knox decided to give the youngster a start and see he could back up in deeds the many words that had been spewing from the infamous Jaws. So Ron went out there, took command of the offense, and surprised everyone with his poise and his cool under fire.

He completed 14 of 20 passes for 172 yards and had a hand in all three L.A. touchdowns as the Rams won, 24-21. He was intercepted once and quickly acknowledged it was his fault and he should have thrown that ball out of bounds. He picked up the Cleveland blitz several times and beat it once for a 20-yard gain to halfback John Cappelletti. Afterward, he was quite pleased with his performance.

"I've been telling people for more than a year that I could play quarterback for the Rams," he said. "So if I had fallen on my face when I got a chance, I would have seemed ridiculous. But I feel I'm 100 percent better than I was last year. I've learned quite a bit, like reading defenses, things like that. I always knew I could throw, but I wasn't so sure about some of the other things."

Ron was being realistic in spite of his propensity for self-promotion. "Every bit of experience helps," he added, "and I know from watching last year that different teams will have different combinations on defense, and that each team varies with the quality of their defensive personnel."

Coach Knox and his staff were quite pleased by the play of the young quarterback.

"Ron showed good poise, threw the ball well, and was a good leader out there," Knox said. "I thought he did a fine job." Then asked whether Ron had a chance to stay on the roster and maybe replace Harris as backup, the coach answered, "Any job on this club is open at any time to the men who can make it."

When the regular season began, the Ram coaches decided to keep three signal-callers on the roster. So Ron was in uniform for the games, though theoretically he was still the number three man behind Hadl and Harris, and number three quarterbacks do not get to play much if at all.

The team did not get off to a flying start in '74, but they were holding their own and the other teams in their division were not all that strong. Yet five games into the season, the front office made a shocking and surprise move. Without warning, they traded John Hadl, who had been so outstanding the year before, and handed the quarterback job to James Harris. Perhaps they felt that Hadl, at age 36, was losing it. But Harris had never proved he had it.

Drafted by Buffalo in 1969, Harris became the first black quarterback to open a season as a starter for an NFL team. He didn't play badly, but didn't set the league ablaze, either. In 1972, the Bills apparently gave up on him as the quarterback of their future and shipped him to L.A. Now he was being given a job on a team noted for devouring quarterbacks. But he felt he was ready, and as a secondary result of the move, Ron suddenly found himself moved into the number two spot. He was sorry to see his good friend John Hadl leave, but he also knew there was now a much greater chance of his seeing some action.

Harris did much better than anyone expected. With a powerful team around him, the big quarterback proved a fine thrower and a tough runner when he had to be.

The club finished at 10-4 to take another divisional title. This time they won their first playoff game, beating Washington, 19-10, but in the NFC title game, they lost to the Minnesota Vikings by the score of 14-10.

With Harris seeing the bulk of the action, Ron got in just five games, mostly at the tail end. He threw just 24 passes and completed 10 for 144 yards. It proved virtually nothing about his ability and just served to frustrate him even more.

The Rams were loaded with talent again in 1975, and once again James Harris was the quarterback. The team began winning and winning big, and Harris was near the top of the NFC pass ratings all year long. Meanwhile Ron sat the bench and fumed. This was his third year and he know he could play. He didn't think he could take this much longer.

Ron had played even less than in '74, when, with two games left, Harris went down. He finally got a chance to start, won the final two games of the year, giving the Rams a 12-2 record and another divisional title. On the season, he completed just 24 of 48 passes for 302 yards. He still hadn't thrown a touchdown pass in NFL competition. Harris, on the other hand, had completed 157 of 385 passes for a 55.1 percent and 2,148 yards. He had thrown for 14 TD's. It was hard to really knock his performance.

But Harris was still unable to go when the Rams met the St. Louis Cardinals in the first game of the playoffs that year. Once again Ron played almost flawless football. He followed the game plan which was somewhat conservative, but the ground game was working, he threw well, and the defense contributed mightily. The Rams won the game, 35-23, and moved into the NFC title game once more, this time against Dallas.

It was probably right here that Ron soured on Los Angeles for the final time. He felt, that with three straight wins under his belt as a starter, and with the momentum going for him and the offensive unit, he would naturally get the start against Dallas. As a rule of thumb, a team will go with the hot man.

But it wasn't to be. With Harris' injury healed, he got the call against Dallas and Ron did a slow burn, which grew worse as the game wore on. The Cowboys were running all over the field against the Rams, and they wound up by inflicting L.A. with a humiliating, 37-7, defeat. The team had been stopped a step short of the Super Bowl once again.

The Rams knew that Ron was angry and disappointed about not getting a start against Dallas, and they promised him a full shot at the starting job in the 1976 preseason. But before camp began, the situation became even more complex. The Rams picked up another quarterback, Pat Haden, who had been an All-American at the University of Southern California, as well as a Rhodes Scholar. In 1975, Haden had played quarterback in the new World Football League, because they allowed him to leave the team early in order to study at Oxford in England.

But in '76, Haden decided to join the Rams. He was the favorite son, the local boy, who had made his reputation on the west coast. Right away, many Rams fans wanted him to be the team's quarterback. It was rapidly turning into a messy situation. Ron kept popping off. He was telling everyone who could listen that he was a Super Bowl quarterback and could get the team there if they would just give him the chance. By now he wasn't really getting along well with some of the L.A. press and didn't always have good things to say about the fans.

"The fans were great for jumping on your bandwagon when you were doing good, then getting on your case when you made a mistake," he said. "Rams' fans don't come to the Coliseum for a football game. They come all dressed up for a fashion show."

At the same time, James Harris was complaining. He pointed out that he was 17-4 as a starter and still had no guarantees about starting. He said part of the problem was racial.

"I'm just not as accepted . . . because I'm a black quarterback," he told one writer. "I've started the last two seasons and I've had statistics comparable to Tarkenton or Staubach or Kilmer. Then all I hear in the off-season is that the Rams are weak at quarterback, and that the jury is still out on James Harris."

To his credit, Harris performed brilliantly in the pre-season and seemed to have the top job sewed up once more. Then, in the next to last exhibition game, he threw a long, 60-yard touchdown bomb. But in following through, his passing hand slammed into the helmet of a changing lineman. He cracked a bone at the base of his thumb. Suddenly, he was on the shelf for at least a month.

Without warning and after three seasons in the wings, the quarterback job suddenly belonged to Ron. He certainly hadn't wished any ill on Harris, but if it had to be, he wasn't going to blow it. He played well in the final exhibition, with Haden relieving him at the end. Then he was named the starting quarterback in the season opener against Atlanta. At last.

It was a close game in the opening quarter. Ron was playing well and leading the Rams on the long drive toward the Falcons goal line. The game plan called for mostly ground plays, and runners Lawrence McCutcheon and John Cappelletti were doing the job. But with the ball in close, Ron decided to keep it himself. Taking the snap, he hurtled across the goal line, but got up his was holding his right shoulder. He was in obvious pain.

He had to leave the game as Haden came in. Later, he

received the bad news. With his first chance ever to run the team on a sustained basis, he had fractured his shoulder. It was a bitter blow. So in the very first game of the 1976 season, the third string quarterback was in making his pitch for the number one job.

Haden helped the team win its opener, then quarterbacked a 10-10 tie with the Vikings a week later. But the next week Harris was back with a bandaged thumb. Though not as sharp as in the preseason, he quarterbacked a pair of victories before having a terrible game against San Francisco on a Monday night. He also hurt a shoulder and the next week against Chicago, Haden was back. He had the club out in front, 10-0, when he was hit hard and knocked dizzy.

Suddenly, Ron was trotting back onto the field. Still rusty from the injury, two of his first six passes were picked off, the other four incomplete. In fact, his first throw was a bomb to Harold Jackson and Ron actually thought it was going to go for a score.

"I was walking off the field and counting the points," he said, later. Then I saw Harold slow down. I said, 'Run, Harold!' But the ball fell off his hands. And I thought, what did I do to deserve that!"

In fact, both the intercepts caromed off receivers' hands. In the second half, the entire Ram offense seemed out of sync. But the defense held up and their overall talent prevailed. Late in the game Ron completed a bomb to Ron Jessie which led to the final field goal, making it a 20-12 Ram victory.

After the game, all three Ram quarterbacks said they felt they would be ready the following week, and it would be up to the coaches to pick the starter. But Ron, as usual, had more to say. He wasn't happy.

"Before the game, I was disappointed that I wasn't starting, but once we got it going in the second half, it felt great. I don't know who will start next week, but I'm ready. Still, I don't think the quarterback situation will ever be solved here, and it's the uncertainty that makes it difficult. But I'll be ready."

The game of musical quarterbacks was becoming almost a guessing game among the writers and fans. And Ron was getting more vocal in his criticism of team policies.

"This isn't a passing team," he said. "It's a ball-control team that wins with defense. There's so much talent here that we don't need a quarterback to win for us. All the quarterback has to do is make sure he doesn't lose it for us. There's no doubt in my mind that this team can win most of its games with almost any quarterback."

Ron did get the start against New Orleans the following week, and this time he didn't play well. Then it was Harris' turn again. The whole thing was turning into a joke. Finally, with five games left, the coaches made a decision. They said that for the good of the entire team there had to be just one number one quarterback. And their choice: Pat Haden!

So once again Ron was relegated to the bench, and in his mind he knew right there his days in L.A. were over. He wasn't sure how he'd do it, but he knew he had to get out, go somewhere else if he wanted to be a first string quarterback and attempt to play up to the potential he still knew he had.

With Haden at the controls down the stretch, the Rams finished at 10-3-1 to take still another NFC West crown. Then a familiar pattern emerged. The team won its first playoff game with Dallas, 14-12, but once again lost the NFC title game, this time to Minnesota, 24-13. The team just could not get over that final hurdle and get to the Super Bowl.

But none of this really concerned Ron now. He had had another mini-season, as far as he was concerned. He completed only 20 of 52 passes for 273 yards, one score, and five intercepts. His passing percentage of 28.5 was abominable. He just couldn't go through it again. Even his wife knew it was over in L. A.

"After the 1976 season we both knew we couldn't stay there anymore," Liz Jaworski said. "I could see how much Ron was hurt mentally by the way the team was using him. He would come home on Friday really down because after working with the first unit all week, they'd tell him he wasn't going to start. It was very, very hard for us and I'm just glad he had the courage to play out his option."

That's what Ron was in the process of doing. He had reportedly been offered a five-year pact during training camp, calling for an estimated $700,000. But Ron said no. He wanted to see if he would win the starting job. Then when the fun and games, and injuries of the season became a reality, he definitely decided to play out the option.

In March of 1977, just a few weeks before becoming a free agent, and with rumors circulating that he was going to sign with San Diego, the Rams decided to move him. They announced they were sending him to the Philadelphia Eagles for a disgruntled tight end named Charles Young.

At first, Ron wasn't sure what to think. He knew the Eagles were not a good team, coming off a pair of 4-10 seasons. But he also knew that they had a dynamic young coach, one who he knew. It was Dick Vermeil, who had been the QB coach at L.A. in 1973. Then, after two successful years at UCLA, Vermeil went to Philly, where he promised to revitalize the franchise.

The incumbent quarterbacks in March of 1977 were Roman Gabriel, now aging and operating on bad legs, and Mike Boryla, who hadn't shown enough to warrant long-term consideration. When Ron went to meet with Vermeil he received an unexpected and very pleasant surprise. He was handed the Eagles quarterback job. . .

and not just until he had one bad game.

"I wanted Ron," said Vermeil. "I knew he had a lot to learn, but I really believed he had a great career ahead of him. I told him he was my quarterback. And I said to him, 'You're going to play on your bad days until they become your good days. It may cost us three bad games in a row but you're going to start and play, no matter what.' "

Ron couldn't believe his ears. He was being told in one breath that the job was his, he didn't even have to earn it, and that it was his period. There wasn't even the slightest suggestion that he was on trial. It was just a total vote of confidence. We know you're the man and we'll stick with you."

The Eagles then showed their good faith with something more tangible, a series of five, one-year contracts said to be worth in the neighborhood of $850,000. It was like a dream come true.

"It was an incredible feeling," he said. "My God, I was finally at peace with the world, getting the chance to do the one thing I wanted in life, to play quarterback in the National Football League. I knew the team was looking to me for leadership, and I also knew that if I made a mistake or two, I was not going to be banished to the bench."

Ron knew the Eagles had been a losing team for a long time. He figured he'd have to work to help get rid of the team's losing attitude. He quickly found he had a perfect ally in Dick Vermeil. The coach had the same kind of positive attitude that Ron had, and wasn't ashamed of it. He was also perhaps the hardest working coach in the league and he expected a lot from his players. Ron found they were already working for him.

"I found guys working hard in the weight room and it was still the off-season," Ron recalls. "They were really serious about it, really pumping iron. I could see that the coach had already instilled a winning attitude in them."

It wasn't long before Ron was extremely excited about the upcoming season. Once he became comfortable with his new surroundings and the writers discovered him, he began talking as only Ron Jaworski can. But his confidence was refreshing and realistic at the same time.

"I'm not gonna kid anybody and say we're gonna win fourteen straight games this year," he said. "And we aren't going to win the Super Bowl. But we are gonna take that first big step and establish a winning attitude. And I don't mean just among the players. I mean among the fans and the news media, as well. By the time this year is over, people won't be coming to Veterans Stadium, say, "Oh, well, I wonder how they're gonna blow this one?' Rather they'll be saying, 'I wonder how they're gonna pull it out this week.

"This is a very close-knit team and there's a good feeling around here. We all feel as if big things are just around the corner and I'm happy to be part of it. For four years I had people in Los Angeles patting me on the back, telling me I was 'the quarterback of the future.' A guy can waste a career that way.

"Hey, I don't want to be put on a shelf and aged like a bottle of imported wine. Pop my cork, man. I want to play. And I don't care if it takes us five years or ten years. Mark my words, someday this team is going to be in the Super Bowl."

In spite of their losing records in recent years, the Eagles under Vermeil were beginning to acquire some fine ballplayers. The club already had a trio of fine pass receivers. On the outside were Charles Smith and big, 6'-8" Harold Carmichael. The tight end was the improving Keith Krepfle. While the running game had been spotty, a sixth-round draft choice in 1977, Wilbert Montgomery, would become a superstar beginning in

1978. The offensive line had some fine players who were beginning to come together as a unit.

Defensively, the team was also improving. End Carl Hairston was already there and tackle Charlie Johnson was a seventh round choice in '77. The great middle line-backer Bill Bergey had joined the team in 1974 and John Bunting in 1972. Cornerback Herman Edwards arrived as a free agent in 1977 and safety Randy Logan arrived in 1973. These were all players, who, with others coming later, would contribute significantly to the rise of the Eagles under Dick Vermeil.

The excitement was building already in 1977. The fans were starved for a winner and before the season even began some 60,000 season tickets (the stadium held 66,000) had already been sold.

"One reporter told me that if we go 7-7, I could run for Mayor," Ron said. "If I went 7-7 in L.A., they'd run me out of town. It's really amazing."

The first pre-season game that year was against the New York Jets. Ron played the first half and hit on nine of 16 passes for 176 yards as the Eagles won, 21-3. Already, his new teammates liked having him around.

"Ron is so positive," said Harold Carmichael. "He just oozes confidence. When he gets in the huddle, you feel like, 'Hey, here we go.' "

The club finished the pre-season with a 3-3 record and showed some fine promise for the upcoming year. It also showed that Ron Jaworski was ready to assume full command of the offense. Sure, he made mistakes and Coach Vermeil knew he would have to work very hard with the quarterback. But he also felt he had done the right thing in acquiring Ron and making him his quarterback now and for the future.

On paper, the 1977 season showed only a one-game improvement over the previous two seasons. The Eagles finished at 5-9, tied for fourth and fifth in the division with the New York Giants. But there were so many small, subtle improvements that no one was really disappointed, not even the fans, at least those who knew something about the game.

For one thing, the club fielded a much improved defense. Defensive coordinator Marion Campbell installed a 3-4, meaning three down linemen and four linebackers, and it worked well. In fourteen games, the defense allowed just 207 points, a club record for a fourteen-game slate. In the past two seasons the defense had yielded 302 and 286 points respectively. The team's victories came over Tampa Bay, the Giants twice, the Saints and New York Jets.

However, there were some close ones, like a 17-13 loss to the Lions, a 21-17 defeat by the Cards, a 16-10 loss to the Cowboys, 23-17 to the Redskins, 17-14 to the Redskins, 21-16 again to the Cards, 14-6 to the Patriots. If the team had won just two of those they would have had a .500 season. Had they won three, they would have been winners at 8-6. So, considering the closeness of those seven games, the team did not miss by much going over the hump.

As for Ron, he was finally a starting quarterback and he went all the way, getting the call in every game. And considering it was his first full season, he didn't do badly at all. He hit on 166 of 346 passes for 2,183 yards. His completion percentage of 48.0 could be improved upon and he had to cut down on his 21 interceptions. But he did throw for eighteen touchdowns and showed the ability to strike from anywhere on the field. He was also forming an incredibly close working relationship with Dick Vermeil.

"Ron was the kind of quarterback I could relate to," said the coach. "He wanted to learn, he wanted to get better. He was receptive to coaching and wasn't afraid to work. He was cocky, but he was realistic, too. He knew he had some growing up to do. I knew we weren't going to do it all at once. We had to upgrade our overall personnel and I knew Ron would make his share of mistakes. But I also knew he was our future, the guy we had to build on."

And Ron confirmed that their relationship that first year or so went beyond the usual X's and O's.

"Most people don't know this," he said, "but I spent many nights in Dick's office when he would really chew me out. It wasn't only about football, but about life, about my attitudes in general.

"Since my father had died in 1971, I didn't have all that much discipline through college and maybe I became too much of a free spirit because of the situation in L.A. I talked too much, fooled around too much. Dick grabbed me by the seat of my pants and pulled me back down to earth."

And there was also plenty of work to be done on the football front. One of Ron's big mistakes was allowing his powerful arm to do too much. Many times he overthrew an open target by simply putting too much mustard on the throw. As one writer put it, "he missed the big play when it was there and tried to force it when it wasn't."

Ron admitted as much, saying that he often got very excited when he saw a receiver break free deep, and his arm would tighten and he would overthrow.

"I'm learning to feather the ball, laying it out there and letting the guy run under it rather than throwing on a line," he said. "I'm also discovering that there are situations when you have to go for the big play and situations where you have to go for three or four yards. Early in the year I forced too much and paid for it. That was probably my biggest negative. I still like to go for the big play, for six points instead of six yards if the defense allows it. But maybe last year teams baited me into trying for the big play because of my personality.

"What I want to achieve is the total confidence of my teammates. I want them to feel that in a tough situation they can look to me and I'll come through. We've got to feel we're as good as the Cowboys, the Redskins, the Cardinals, and then prove it by going out there and beating them. Maybe we have been putting these teams on a pedestal; maybe we gave them too much respect.

"We had a lot of them beat last year, had two strikes on them and let them get away. I really think the way we looked up to them had some bearing on why we lost."

Coach Vermeil wanted to be sure Ron didn't make a lot of the same mistakes in 1978. So what he did was put together a film reel of all Ron's interceptions and near interceptions. The two then spent hours and hours together, looking at the films over and over, with Vermeil questioning the quarterback on the purpose of the play, the situation, and why he did what he did.

"It was painful," Ron admits, "sitting there and watching yourself make mistake after mistake. But I learned my lesson. That cliché about taking what the defense gives you is really the truth."

In 1978, the Eagles looked to get over that hump. Some more fine players arrived to give the team both starters and quality depth. They included halfbacks Billy Campfield and Louie Giammona, defensive end Dennis Harrison, cornerback Bob Howard, veteran guard Woody Peoples, and linebacker Reggie Wilkes. Plus running back Wilbert Montgomery was about to become one of the most feared players in the league.

Ron, too, was anxious to get started. "I feel a lot more relaxed coming into camp this year," he said. "I satisfied a lot of my own goals last year, but I've set even higher ones this time around. I won't say what all of them are but I want to be more of a high-percentage passer and cut down on interceptions."

If anything, the coach's opinion of Ron had escalated. "When last season ended," Vermeil said, "I thought Ron Jaworski was good. But after watching films of him all off-season, now I'm more convinced than ever that he's going to be a superstar."

Ron was not coming into the 1978 season completely healthy. He had injured his left wrist in the next to last game of 1977. By April, when it was still bothering him, X-rays revealed a fracture. The wrist wouldn't be right all year, but Ron rarely complains. In fact, he had a hairline fracture of the right thumb the second half of '77 and continued to play with the pain.

The opening game was a heartbreaking loss for both Ron and the Eagles. For one thing, it was against Ron's old team, the Rams. And for the other, the Eagles had a 14-13 lead going into the final minutes when the Rams' Frank Corral booted a 46-yard field goal to win it. Ron was just seven of 17, following a conservative game plan, and some fans at Veterans Memorial Stadium were booing. They wanted to see more wide open football, especially with the Polish Rifle at the helm.

When they lost another close one, 35-30, to the Redskins the following week, it looked like 1977 all over again. It's said that teams that have been losing for a long time must *learn* how to win all over again. And until they do, they always manage to lose the close ones. That could be the case with the Eagles.

But then the club began winning. They whipped New Orleans, 24-17, and Miami, 17-3. Then they knocked off Baltimore, 17-14, before losing to tough New England, 24-14. They beat Washington, 17-10, then lost two key games, and again by very close scores. The Cowboys took them, 14-7, and St. Louis triumphed, 16-10. After nine games the team stood at 4-5. They had hoped to do better, but still saw progress.

One of those definitely doing better was Ron

Jaworski. He was up near the top of the NFC passers, completing nearly 55 percent of his throws and cutting his intercepts to seven, so far. Those were two of the areas in which he wanted to improve, and he had.

"I've always been a very competitive person and this year I'm learning to control it," he said. "I always wanted to be the guy on the foul line with one second left and my team trailing by one, or the guy on the 18th green with a 10-foot putt needed to win.

"I really love facing that kind of pressure. It really excites me. But it can hurt you if you can't control it. This year I feel I'm picking my spots, I'm more calculating. Self-confidence is something I never lacked, but now I'm gaining maturity to go with it."

The team still played a ball control game. Wilbert Montgomery was rushing toward 1,000 yards and the team didn't throw as much as some of the other clubs. In fact, when they threw more they got in trouble. For instance, coming into game nine with St. Louis, Ron had been picked off just four times. But Montgomery and three other running backs were hurt and Ron put the ball up 40 times, completing 23 for 231 yards and a score. But three were picked off and St. Louis won the game. Yet Coach Vermeil didn't fault Ron, in fact, he praised him.

"Ron has the amazing ability to keep battling right until the end of the game," the coach said. "That's a great quality. He did some great things in rallying us back with a limited attack. I don't like to throw forty times a game, but against the Cardinals we had to."

After a 10-3 victory over the Packers, the Eagles went up against the New York Jets. Ron had a fine game, hitting 13 of 23 for 135 yards and two scores. But the score was just 10-9, Eagles, with less than two minutes to play. Ron had engineered a time-consuming drive that brought the ball down to the six-yard line. From there, he threw a perfect pass to big Harold Charmichael for the clinching touchdown.

But just as Ron released the ball, Jets linebacker Mike Hennigan hit the QB in the back, helmet first. Ron went down like a shot, writhing in pain. His back had gone into spasms and he had to be carried from the field. The Eagles players feared he would be out of action.

"I'll be fine," Ron said. "I don't think it was a late hit, but I don't really remember. All I know is it hurts when I breathe. I never had spasms like that before and it was a rather eerie, frightening feeling."

Such is the life of an NFL quarterback. A week later he was back on the job and the club won its third straight, defeating the Giants, 19-17. Then they made it four, finally overcoming the Cardinals, 14-10. They were suddenly a winning team at 8-5 and had an outside shot at a wildcard berth in the playoffs.

A close, 28-27, loss to the Vikings hurt, and so did a 31-13 shellacking by the Cowboys. With an 8-7 record, the club now had to beat the Giants in the finale to make the playoffs. Ron told the press that there was no way the Giants could win with Randy Dean (a backup) at quarterback. His teammates didn't appreciate the remark, since it could easily give Dean and the Giants the incentive to try harder. Ron admitted the Jaws had worked overtime. In fact, this was one of the remarks that got him the new nickname of "Dial-a-Quote."

"I've never been one to hold anything back," he said, "but believe it or not I'm trying to control myself more. I realize one of my problems is not being able to keep my mouth shut. In fact, Dick (Vermeil) considers it one of my major faults."

Fortunately, the Giants just didn't have the personnel to make much of a fight. Philly won easily, 20-3, to finish at 9-7 for the season and make it into the playoffs. It was an exciting moment for the team, which hadn't had a winning season since 1966.

Ron, of course, led a balanced attack that saw Wilbert Montgomery set a new Eagles record with 1,220 yards on 259 carries. Carmichael caught 55 passes for 1,072 yards, while tight end Krepfle had 26 for 374. Montgomery, incidentally, was also an outstanding receiver with 34 catches.

As for Ron, he had his finest year yet, with 206 completions in 398 attempts for a 51.8 percentage and 2,487 yards. He threw for 16 touchdowns and had the same number intercepted. He had done a fine job.

In the first round of the playoffs the Eagles had to meet another wildcard team, the Atlanta Falcons. It turned into a big disappointment for Eagle fans. Despite blowing numerous other chances, the Eagles still held a 13-0 lead well into the final period. Yet they had missed an extra point, a couple of TD opportunities, and a couple of field goals.

Finally, Atlanta got on the scoreboard to make it 13-7. When the Eagles couldn't move, the Falcons got it back, deep in their own territory. But a penalty hurt the Eagles, and with very little time left, Falcon QB Steve Bartkowski hit Wallace Francis from 37 yards out for the winning score. There was one more disappointment when the Eagles kicker missed a 34-yard field goal try with 17 seconds left that could have won it.

Once the immediate disappointment wore off, the Eagles were still proud of their season and vowed to be even better in '79. And, indeed, they seemed to be an up-and-coming team.

Ron had some of his own business to take care of in the off season. It turned out that he needed surgery on his damaged left wrist. He had played in pain all season long, but never allowed it to affect his performance. The operation called for a small piece of bone from his hip area to be grafted into the wrist. It was not that serious an operation.

The Eagles continued to be a portrait of a team on the rise. Some of the new players added in 1979 were wide receiver Scott Fitzkee, placekicker Tony Franklin, fullback Leroy Harris, veteran defensive end Claude Humphrey, guard Pete Perot, linebacker Jerry Robinson, punter Max Runager, tight end John Spagnola, and safety Brenard Wilson. Coach Vermeil wasn't kidding when he said he wanted to upgrade the personnel. He was building a powerful, balanced, and very deep team. And by now, the player the Eagles could least afford to lose was Ron Jaworski.

So they were at it again, opening at home against the rival Giants. The New Yorkers took a lead on a field goal in the first, then the Eagles exploded. First Billy Campfield ran a yard for a score. Then Ron passed seven yards to Carmichael. Minutes later he hit the tall receiver from 41 yards out for a second score. A 46-yard field goal by Franklin made it 23-3 at the half. From there, Philly hung on for a 23-17 victory. Ron opened his season with 12 of 21 for 186 yards.

Atlanta then shut down Philly's running game and repeated their triumph from the playoffs. This time it was 14-10, as Ron passed 37 times, completing 16 for 213 yards. As the coach said, that's too much passing to win. But the club rebounded to beat New Orleans and the Giants again.

Then came a big one. The club proved it could play with the best by beating defending Super Bowl champ Pittsburgh, 17-14. A ten-point third period did it with an interception setting up the winning score. Then with wins over Washington and St. Louis, the team upped its record to 6-1. It looked as if they finally had arrived. But just as suddenly the club ran into trouble.

First Washington beat them, 17-7, as the running

game was stopped and Ron was sacked seven times and pressured on numerous other occasions by a furious Redskin pass-rush. Cincinnati turned the trick the next week, 37-13, as the Eagles turned the ball over four times inside their own 30 and the Bengals capitalized with three touchdowns and a field goal. Playing catch-up, Ron had a mediocre day with 11 of 21 for 112 yards.

The next one was a heartbreaker. Cleveland beat the Eagles, 24-19, despite a sensational 197-yard rushing day by Montgomery and a 16-23, 205-yard day from Ron. Two, fourth-period Browns touchdowns did the trick, and the team had come back to 6-4, with a pivotal game coming up against Dallas.

It was a Monday night game and Dallas scored in the first 61 seconds on a 48-yard TD pass from Roger Staubach to Tony Hill. It looked as if the Eagles mettle would be tested early. Ron accepted the challenge, moved his team downfield, and connected with Carmichael for a 32-yard scoring toss that knotted the game at 7-7.

Ron was shaken up early in the second period and backup John Walton came in to throw a 29-yard TDer to Charlie Smith. Then, Franklin, a barefooted kicker from Texas A & M booted a 59-yard field goal to give the Eagles a 17-7 lead at the half. Ron was back in the third session and hit Carmichael from 13 yards out to make it 24-7. In the fourth period, the Cowboys rallied to draw to 24-21, but Montgomery broke free on a 37-yard scoring run to put the game on ice. Philly won, 31-21, clearing a major hurdle.

The next week it was St. Louis, and the Cards held a 13-9 lead in the final quarter. But with the game on the line, Ron hit tight end Keith Krepfle on a 40-yard scoring pass to win the game, 16-13. With Montgomery headed for another big year, Ron wasn't throwing that much again. Plus he was only completing about 50 percent of his passes, but he was making the big play time and again, and winning ballgames with it.

Green Bay fell next, then Detroit, as Ron hit 14 of 23 for 233 yards and a pair of scoring tosses to Carmichael. The team was now 10-4 and battling Dallas for the NFC East lead. That's why a 24-17 loss to the Cowboys hurt. Ron had 216 yards to just 105 for Roger Staubach, but Dallas still won by the margin of a touchdown.

A win over Houston, 26-20, in the final game gave the club an 11-5 mark for the year, the same as Dallas, but the Cowboys took the division title because of the NFL tiebreaking system. Philly was in the playoffs again, but once more as a wildcard.

It was another fine year for all the Eagles stars, especially Montgomery, now one of the finest backs in the game. He had 1,512 yards on 338 carries and an additional 41 receptions for another 494 yards, a great season.

With Wilbert running so often, Ron didn't throw as much as he had in '78. He completed just 190 of 374 for 50.8 percent, those figures all down slightly from the year before. But he threw for more yardage, 2,669, more touchdowns with 18, and fewer intercepts with 12. So he put in another fine season. He still felt he was making progress and gave more credit to his coach.

"Dick made me into a quarterback," Ron said. "Before I came here I was a run-and-gun guy. I was always swinging for the fences. I'd have a guy wide open in the flat and throw into double coverage forty yards downfield. I thought I was being aggressive, but I was just being dumb.

"It was Dick who harnessed my energy. He put me in an offense he conceived. He called the plays and he brought me along at his pace. There were times when I felt like busting loose, really airing it out, but I knew if

I did that I'd only be regressing."

The wildcard game in the NFC in '79 was between the Eagles and Chicago Bears. Philly scored first when Ron hit Carmichael from 17, but the Bears came back on a Walter Payton run to make it 7-7 at the half. The Eagles then began playing poorly, allowing the Bears to make it 17-10, at the half.

In the third period the Eagles were still struggling, and when Ron threw an interception early in the session, the fans booed him as he left the field.

"Don't listen to 'em, Jaws," said Harold Carmichael. "They'll be on their feet before the day is over."

Next time on, Ron drove the Eagles 77 yards on six plays, hitting Carmichael for the tying score from 29 out. Then early in the fourth period he had a third and 15 on his own 15. With his receivers covered, he took off and ran up the middle for 20 yards and a first down. Minutes later, with a third and eight on his own 37, he cranked up and hit Billy Campfield down the sideline. Campfield took off and turned it into a 67-yard TD pass-run to put the game away. A Franklin field goal made the final, 27-17.

Ron had hit on 12 of 23 for 204 yards, but it had been one of the first times he had ever been booed in Philly.

"Don't tell the fans this," Ron quipped afterward. "But I think the booing motivated us. When they started in on me, I know I vowed to do better. I never felt it was out of hand, even when we were behind."

But there was no time to rest on laurels. Now the Eagles had to travel to Florida to face the Tampa Bay Buccaneers. And suddenly, it all ended. The Bucs moved to a 17-7 halftime lead and were never headed, hanging on with their great defense for a 24-17 triumph. Ron tried to get the Eagles back, hitting 15 of 38 for 199 yards, a pair of scores, and no intercepts. But it seemed whenever he threw so many passes, the team lost. This one was no exception. It would be wait till next year once again.

When Ron began throwing again the following May, he made a startling admission to reporters.

"We were going with just two quarterbacks in training camp last year and we had to do all the throwing," he said. "I think that took something out of my arm. I didn't really feel I had good zip on the ball for most of the season. It wasn't something Dick knew about, or anyone for that matter. Just something I felt.

"I don't think it affected the distance on my throws. Most of the time you don't throw as far as you can anyway. But throwing off-balance, when you've got to arm-throw it, that's when I felt it."

So Ron rested the arm more in the off-season and was more careful in camp. He wanted to take his club over that final hump, and although he didn't say it, he probably felt he had to produce a better season to do it. He and Coach Vermeil continued to work very hard together. In their regular weekly routine, Ron said Wednesday was the toughest day, with all-day meetings and then taking films home to watch at night, studying the defensive alignments of the Eagles' next opponent.

"Sometimes I'm confused by what I see," he said. "There have been plenty of times when I've called Dick at 11 p.m. or even midnight, and we talk. He tells me what he's seen in the films and what he thinks."

By now the club was pretty well established. Joe Pisarcik, formerly with the Giants, was the new back-up quarterback, and there were solid players at all the positions. Most people felt that 1980 would be the year the Eagles made it to the Super Bowl. It was important to everyone, especially Ron.

"I've looked back over the careers of guys like Staubach and Terry Bradshaw," he said, "and there is one thing constant in their images. They were not recognized as great quarterbacks until they won, and I mean the Super Bowl. It's rather obvious to me that the way to become a great quarterback is to have a great team. In past seasons I outlined some personal goals. I haven't done that this year, because the only thing I want to do is win."

The Eagles opened the 1980 season as if they all had the same thing in mind. Playing a very good Denver Broncos team, Philly wasted no time setting the tone for the season. Early in the first period Ron cranked up and found Harold Carmichael open for a 56-yard scoring toss. In the second period he hit Scott Fitzkee from 16 yards out, and Franklin added a field goal to make it 20-0. Ron added another scoring pass to John Spagnola in the final session, making the final, 27-6.

What a debut for Ron and the offense. He hit on 18 of 29 passes for 281 yards and three scores. Montgomery chipped in with 71 yards rushing and six passes caught, and big Carmichael snagged three for 135 yards. It was an awesome offensive display.

A week later they were at it again. Playing another good team, the Minnesota Vikings, the Eagles struck early, Leroy Harris going in from the two, and Wilbert Montgomery from the 72. It was 14-0 at the end of one. The same two runners scored in the third session, and in the final, Ron hit Fitzkee from 45-yards out and Carmichael from 13. Plus his passing had set up the earlier scores. The final was 42-7. Montgomery had 169 yards and Ron was 20-26 for 234 yards. After two games, Ron was the NFL's leading passer, hitting 66.7 percent of his throws and five scores with just one intercept.

Week number three was a Monday night special against the Giants. The Eagle machine continued to roll, this time by a 35-3 count. Ron had another big night, 18 of 29 for 240 yards. But the following Sunday the bubble burst. St. Louis surprised the Eagles with a 24-14 upset. Cardinal Ottis Anderson had 151 yards, while Ron was erratic. He had 231 yards, but only on a 16 for 36 night, and three of his passes were picked off.

Worse news was the loss of Wilbert Montgomery for a couple of weeks with a hip pointer. Ron said after the game, "Coach Vermeil never said he expected us to finish at 16-0."

Against Washington the following week, the club rebounded. The defense played a fine game and Ron threw for 193 yards and two touchdowns as the team won it, 24-14. Montgomery surprised everyone by playing and gaining 41 yards. The Giants fell the next week as Ron's pinpoint passing accounted for 18 of 28 for 212 yards. The team was tied with Dallas at 5-1, and Ron had thrown for more yardage than any other quarterback in the NFC.

Then in the first big one of the year, the Eagles took the measure of the Cowboys, 17-10, in a game marked by great defensive play. Ron's 15-yard scoring pass to Charlie Smith in the final period broke a 10-all tie and proved the game-winner. Montgomery got hurt again, straining a knee, but Ron threw to 214 yards to take up the slack.

The halfway game was tough. Philly beat the Bears, 17-14, on a Franklin field goal with just 2:02 left. But Ron left with a slight concussion and neither team could generate that much offense. Still, the team was 7-1 and on top. A week later they topped the Seahawks, 27-20, as Ron led an 84-yard scoring drive in the final session, hitting on seven of eight for 67 yards on the march to the winning score. In all, he had 19 of 30 for 253. With the team at 8-1, Ron was putting together a great season, throwing more and for better yardage.

The Philly steamroller continued. The next week New

Orleans fell, 34-21 as Ron had the biggest day of his life. He hit on 21 of 32 for 323 yards, three scores, and no intercepts. A week later it was Washington losing, 24-0. The defense had a big day as Ron threw for just 124 yards. If one person faltered, there was someone else to jump in.

Then came the Oakland Raiders, the bad boys from the west. It was scoreless until the third period when Franklin booted a 51-yard field goal. But early in the fourth, the Raiders rebounded on an 86-yard bomb from Jim Plunkett to speedy Cliff Branch. It was a 7-3 game with time running down. The Eagles began their last drive with 6:52 left.

Ron made a nifty move to avoid a sack and then hit fullback Leroy Harris for a 43-yard gain. Seven plays later, Montgomery went into the end zone for the winning score. The final was 10-7, in what had been a bitterly fought game.

There was no let-up in the schedule. The team was 11-1, the best record in the league, but then the high-flying San Diego Chargers derailed the Eagle express, 22-21, taking a 19-0 lead in the first half and withstanding a late Eagle charge. Ron hit on 20 of 31 for 201 yards as he continued to have by far his greatest all around season.

The pesky Falcons did the Eagles in the following week in a topsy-turvy game, 20-17. The club was now 11-3. With the season winding down, they didn't want to lose their momentum. They got it back beating St. Louis, 17-3 as Ron hit 17 of 34 for 236 yards. The club was 12-3 and Dallas was at 11-4. The only way the Cowboys could now win the division was to defeat the Eagles by 25 of more points in the season wrap. They tried hard, taking a 21-0 lead at the half. But Ron took to the air, literally passing his team back in the game. They lost it, but only by a 35-27 count, as Ron hit 18 of 30 for a whopping 331 yards. The club finished at 12-4 and has won the Eastern Division of the NFC.

And what a season it had been for Ron Jaworski. In his seventh season, not counting the year on the taxi squad, he had really come of age. Hitting on 257 of 451 passes, he threw for a career high (by far) of 3,529 yards, completing 57.0 percent of his passes, another career high. He threw for a high of 27 TD's, and had just 12 picked off. He was the top-rated quarterback in the NFC, second only to Brian Sipe of Cleveland in the league. Vermeil had opened it up some more and Ron responded.

He had plenty of help. In spite of his injuries, Montgomery had 778 yards and caught 50 passes. Carmichael grabbed 48, Smith 47, and Krepfle 30. Ron had distributed the goodies very well. In addition, the Philly defense ranked first in the entire NFL, and that an invaluable commodity for any team.

Now came the playoffs. The Minnesota Vikings were the first opponent, and after a close two periods, the Eagles took charge. The Vikes actually led it, 14-7, at the half. But in the final sessions, the Eagle defense took over, recovering three fumbles and intercepting Tommy Kramer five times. They kept giving the ball back to the offense so Jaworski and company could put 24 second-half points on the board. The final was 31-16. Ron threw for 190 yards and Montgomery gained 74 tough ones.

"We're just sixty minutes away from the Super Bowl," crowed Ron, afterward.

And veteran linebacker Frank LeMaster expressed the sentiments of many of the older players.

"It's like a dream," he said. "Five years ago, I would have never imagined we'd be this close to the big one."

That was the year before Ron came. Once Ron arrived, he'd been promising Super Bowl all along. But there was still a major roadblock. Once again the Eagles would have to meet their archrivals, the Dallas Cowboys. It was a frigid and windy day in Philadelphia when the two clubs squared off and obvious from the start it wouldn't be a day for passing. The Eagles had a score when Wilbert Montgomery wasn't sure whether his knee would hold up just two days before the game.

But on the second offensive play of the game, Wilbert showed the knee was fine by bursting up the middle, cutting to the outside and going 42-yards for a score. Dallas tied the game early in the second period, but after that the Philly defense was absolutely magnificent.

Montgomery kept piling up the yardage as Philly got a field goal and a touchdown from Harris in the third, making it 17-7. In the final session Montgomery had a 55-yard run and Franklin eventually nailed another three pointer. That made it 20-7, and the defense nailed it down. It was one of the greatest days in Eagle history. Montgomery had gained 194 yards on 26 carries, while the Eagles as a team had 263 net. Dallas had just 86. Ron was nine of 29 on the windy day, but fortunately, the club didn't want more. They had finally done it. The Eagles were going to the Super Bowl.

The game was played in the Louisiana Superdome on January 25, and the opponent was the Oakland Raiders, a team the Eagles had beaten, 10-7, in the regular season. The Raiders were attempting to become the first wild card team ever to go all the way. They were a rough, tough bunch, operating behind a resurgent quarterback in Jim Plunkett, and they seemed to get stronger throughout the playoffs.

Close observers in the two weeks preceding the game noticed a difference in the two teams. Vermeil was still using his philosophy of work, work, work, and some said the Eagles looked tired, burned out. The Raiders, on the other hand, were loose and cocky. Some of their vets had been to the super game before, in 1977. And that, too, can make a difference. None of the Eagles had been in this tension-filled game before.

It started badly for the Eagles when Ron's first pass was intercepted by Rod Martin, who returned it 17 yards to the Philadelphia 30. Plunkett drove the Raiders close, and then hit wide receiver Cliff Branch with a little two-yard chip shot for the score. The kick made it 7-0.

On the next series Ron drove the Eagles to the Oakland 40. He then sent Carmichael in motion, dropped back, and threw the other way. Receiver Rodney Parker grabbed the ball and took it into the end zone for the apparent tying score. But there was a flag. Carmichael had turned upfield too soon. That put him in illegal motion, and the ball was called back, a big blow.

Late in the period the Raiders had the ball on their own 20. Plunkett rolled as if to scramble, and when the defensive backs started up, he flipped a quick pass to speedy halfback Kenny King, who broke free and outran the Eagles 80 yards for a score. It was 14-0 before the end of the period.

A 30-yard Franklin field goal was all the scoring in the second, but then in the third the Raiders put another ten points up to make it 24-3, and that was, in effect, the ball game. The final was 27-10, Oakland, and the Eagles had been beaten in their final quest. Plunkett was the MVP with 13 of 21 for 261 yards. Ron had 18 for 38 stats, good for 291 yards. But it was catch-up football, which is not the Eagles bag, and he was intercepted three times.

Some of the Raiders thought the Eagles looked like a tired team. Ron didn't come out and say that, but he did comment on the lack of intensity.

"We never got into the flow of the game," he said. "We seemed fired up at the start, but I sensed a lack of emotion as the game went on and it never seemed to get stronger. We usually have a strong second half—a snowball emotional effect—but it just didn't swell up in the second half this time."

It might sound strange for a team to make the long trek to the Super Bowl and come up flat. But there a Super Bowl history of first-time teams losing. Many of them have come back to win it in subsequent years. The Eagles certainly have the personnel to do it. The team has been built carefully and with precision, from the bottom up.

It's not always easy to find just the right players when you're building a team, but Coach Dick Vermeil was sure of what he wanted when he went shopping for a quarterback. He plucked Ron Jaworski from the second-string heap and handed him the job, assuring a relatively untried player that he was his quarterback of the future.

Vermeil kept his word and Jaworski fulfilled the promise. He has gotten better in each of his years as a starter, and at age 30, should still have his peak years ahead of him. From a cocky, bomb-throwing kid, he has developed into a confident, game-winning quarterback.

And don't forget, good old Jaws, or it is Dial-a-Quote, promised the fans of Philadelphia a Super Bowl Victory. That should continue to serve warning on the rest of the league. Ron Jaworski is a man who likes to keep his promises.

Joe Ferguson

Ask yourself this question. What's a nice, quiet kid from Louisiana who loves raising horses, spending time with his friends, and staying away from large crowds doing in the cold of Buffalo, New York, working at his job in front of some 80,000 people and often taking a brutal beating for his troubles?

The answer is simple. If you're Joe Ferguson and you are the quarterback of the Buffalo Bills, this is how and where you earn your living. It's not always easy, and sometimes the rewards are few. In fact, Joe's career with the Bills has been one often wrought with frustration, sometimes to the point where he seriously thought about retiring.

In Joe's early years on the shores of Lake Erie, the Bills had a running back named O.J. Simpson, perhaps the greatest the game has ever known. So in those days Joe's main task was getting the ball to The Juice and letting him do his thing. Sure, there was some passing to keep the defenses honest, but the attack revolved around O.J. and the quarterback was just another member of the team.

Then in O.J.'s later years when he was slowing down, and after he finally left the team, the Bills were chronic losers, and no matter how good a quarterback is, he never gets his due when the team is going down to defeat week after week. And when the opposition is consistently scoring more points than your team, the tendency is to point the finger at the quarterback and then take it from there.

Even when the team posted consecutive 9-5 records in 1973 and '74, most of the credit went to the record-breaking running of Simpson, and very little to the young quarterback who had taken command of the team as a rookie in 1973. And now that the Bills have once again achieved respectability, making the playoffs in 1980 for the first time since '74, people are pointing to the fine job done by Coach Chuck Knox in rebuilding the team, and to some of the fine young players, such as running back Joe Cribbs and wide receiver Jerry Butler. Still, few rave about the now veteran quarterback.

To many, Joe Ferguson is an underrated and unappreciated quarterback. He's never had the big years statistically that some other signal-callers have put together. But that's more a product of the system under which he plays. He doesn't have the great size of a Steve Bartkowski, the rocket arm of a Terry Bradshaw, the hollar-guy attitude of a Bert Jones, or the flamboyant public personality of a Joe Namath. All Joe Ferguson does is go about his job with quiet professional proficiency.

But like other outstanding athletes, the competitive fires burn brightly within, and Joe has often been out there directing his team despite injuries that would have lesser men sitting on the bench. And he does consider the Bills *his* team. When the fingers of blame have pointed and suggestions for a change made, Joe Ferguson has been quick to take exception.

"Stories about a quarterback change over the years always affect me," he admitted. "I want to be thought of as the number one quarterback and I don't like it when people say, 'He's not. Maybe he's not as good as this guy or that guy.'

"I am the number one quarterback and I want to leave here as the number one quarterback. I've never sat on the bench, never, all the way through high school and college, and even when I came here. I arrived at the right time to compete for the starting job. So I can't really say how I'd accept sitting down and I hope I don't have to find out."

Because of his general lack of recognition, his low-key approach to the game, and his penchant for privacy, not too many people really know about Joe Ferguson. Oh, yes, some fans may remember that he was an all-American from Arkansas in the early 1970s and that he went to the Bills from there. But there are other very interesting facts from his past.

For example, not many people know that four current NFL quarterbacks live within 50 miles or so of each other back in Louisiana. That's right. There's Joe, Terry Bradshaw, Bert Jones, and James Harris. In fact, Joe was the quarterback who took over at Woodlawn High in Shreveport, Louisiana, when Terry Bradshaw graduated. It's football country down there, all right, where the gridiron game often grips the imagination of the entire community.

Maybe it's best at this point to go back to the beginning and find out exactly how Joe Ferguson traveled the long road from Shreveport to Buffalo.

Actually, the story doesn't begin in Louisiana. Joe was born in Alvin, Texas, on April 23, 1950. The Fergusons had one other child, a girl, two years older than Joe. Mr. Ferguson was a painting contractor and when Joe was seven years old he moved the family to Shreveport.

Joe was always a small, rather thin boy, but he was interested in sports from the time he was old enough to understand them. And once he came to Louisiana, it was hard not to be interested, especially in football, which was pretty much the national pastime to residents of the area.

When he was old enough, Joe decided he wanted to play his first organized football in the Pee Wee League. The coaches suggested that because of his build he compete in the featherweight division. But to do that, he would have to lose a few pounds. When his parents heard that, they promptly denied him permission to play.

"Joe was so thin then," his mother recalls, "that we couldn't see how he could have lost any weight. It seemed totally ridiculous."

But it wasn't long before Joe was playing both football and baseball, and often competing on the sandlots with the bigger and heavier boys. He learned the art of survival early. The family lived in the Southern Hills neighborhood of Shreveport, and with football the main sport, all the attention was focused on the local high school. Woodlawn was the high school for the Southern Hills section, and to be on the team was an honor for any boy in the neighborhood.

When Joe reached Oak Terrace Junior High School he was already quite a ballplayer, though still painfully thin. Yet he was already a quarterback on the football team and a catcher on the baseball team, positions usually associated with the big, strong kids. He had a real live arm and a quick release in both sports. He could get that ball down to second or into the end zone very quickly. But even though he was competing at the junior high level, his mind was already elsewhere.

"I was wrapped up in Woodlawn football long before I got there," he says, "as was everyone else in Southern Hills. My sister was a couple of years ahead of me and when she got there she became a member of the pep squad. So I was already at all the home games and couldn't wait to get there myself."

Before going any further, it might be best to learn about Woodlawn High itself, and the kind of atmosphere and tradition that young Joe Ferguson would be moving into in 1967.

It was an oil strike way back in 1906 that originally spurred the growth of Shreveport, which is now Louisiana's second largest city. Some say it's only natural that the descendants of the rough and ready people who came there to work would prefer football to the other sports. An illustration of this comes from the Woodlawn principal, J.W. Cook, Jr.

"There's a little town called Haynesville, which is not far from Shreveport," Mr. Cook said, "and they once had a basketball team there which won the district championship. Yet if they had 50 people at the games it was considered a good crowd. Yet at the same time you would have about 150 people out watching the football team practice . . . just practice. No doubt about it, football has always been king in these parts."

Football became a rallying point in the Shreveport area when Centenary College rose to prominence in the 1930s, and pretty soon fierce rivalries were developing right down to the high school level. For a long time there were two high schools for white students, Byrd and Fair Park. Then a school for black students was built, Booker T. Washington. It wasn't until 1960 that Woodlawn was built.

When the new school was designed and constructed, it was obvious that football was to play a prominent role in the overall school life. There were complete and modern facilities, for practice and for the games. Scarlet and royal blue became the colors for the Woodlawn Knights. A.L. Williams was an assistant coach that first year and later became head coach. He remembers how tough it was getting started.

"We didn't win a game that first season," he recalls. "In fact, we didn't score a touchdown until the fourth game, but the fans stuck by us, even though we were losing by 40 or 50 points. We had an incredible following from the beginning and it's never stopped."

It didn't take long for another tradition to start. The second year of the program along came a quarterback named Billy Laird, and he took the team from 0-9 to the district championship. He did it by throwing the football, and the Knights began a tradition of great passing quarterbacks that seemed unending.

After Laird came a youngster named Trey Prather, a 6'-2", 200-pounder who had enormous potential as a thrower.

"Trey was a classic dropback passer with all the tools," recalls A.L. Williams. "He was a classic dropback passer with a great arm and great timing. I think he could have gone on to become a great pro."

But fate had something else in store for Trey Prather. He attender LSU for a year, then enlisted in the army where he was tragically killed in Vietnam. He is still much remembered at Woodlawn and in Southern Hills.

While Prather was still throwing bullets for Woodlawn, another young kid stood waiting for his big chance, which wouldn't come until he was a senior. His name was Terry Bradshaw, and there isn't a football fan in America who doesn't know of him and his accomplishments with the Pittsburgh Steelers.

Terry was a big, raw-boned kid even then. He came to Woodlawn at 170 lbs. and left weighing 190. He was physically imposing, even then, and that season he threw 21 TD passes and led Woodlawn into the State Championship game, only to lose it in a driving rainstorm.

Bradshaw graduated in 1966. Most of the other starters were juniors, so Woodlawn would have a nearly all-senior team in the fall. Only they didn't have a quarterback. That's when Joe Ferguson came to the school as a sophomore and reported to practice, announcing he was a quarterback. Both Trey Prather and Bradshaw were imposing physical specimens, especially for high school kids. But when Joe Ferguson said he was a quarterback, A.L. Williams remembers doing a doubletake.

"When I first saw Joe he must have weighed less than 140 pounds. He was rail thin. Terry had just graduated and we really needed a quarterback. But I looked at him and said, 'This kid just can't do it.' But I gave him a shot in practice and when he threw the ball I couldn't believe it, the strength of his arm for his size and most of all that extremely quick release."

Coach Williams decided he would go with Ferguson as a sophomore. Because Woodlawn had a big, senior team, the emphasis was more on ball control and a running game. But Joe directed the team extremely well and they won 11 straight games before losing to Bogalusa for the state title. He got his baptism under fire, but the veteran club took some of the pressure off him and he only had to put the ball up some 101 times. But the next year would be a different story.

The seniors were gone. In fact, Joe was the only returning starter, and the youngsters joining him seemed smaller and lighter than in past season. In fact, the biggest kid on the team weighed about 190 pounds. It could have been the first Woodlawn team in many years that wasn't really competitive or top notch. Coach Williams decided to rethink his strategy.

"The only way I could see us winning was to go with an all out aerial attack," he said. "So I decided to really turn Joe loose and see what he could do."

Coach Williams would find out in a hurry. The opener was against powerful Airline High, the team that would wind up as state champs that year. On nearly every offensive play, Ferguson dropped back and threw the ball. When the game ended, Woodlawn had a 28-14 upset victory and Joe Ferguson had completed 29 of 48 passes for a host of yardage and three scores. The coach's gambit had worked and in the process he had found another great quarterback to carry on the Wood-lawn tradition.

A week later Joe did the same thing against archrival Byrd, completing 31 of 47 passes for six touchdowns. Woodlawn won easily 40-6, but the following day's headlines read: Ferguson 40, Byrd 6! Coach Williams remembers Joe's reaction:

"Joe asked permission to speak with the team the next day," Williams recalls. "He was practically in tears and he apologized to the team for the newspaper headline, over which he had no control. He was upset because the headline made it appear as if he had won the game sin-gle-handedly. He was really sincere about it and he made such a great impression with his teammates that I think it laid the groundwork for the championship we won the next season."

The Knights went all the way to the state semi-finals that year before losing, as Joe threw 35 touchdown passes to break Bradshaw's record of 21. And when he came back for his senior year of 1968, he was better than ever. He had such a quick release by then that he got the nickname of the "White Knight." His uniform never seemed to get dirty because he got his passes off so quickly the defense never had time to dump him.

In the opener that year against the number one team in the state, Lagrange, Woodlawn trailed, 21-6, right be-fore the half. But Joe uncorked and got two quick scores on the board. He dominated the second half and Wood-lawn won going away, 34-21. Afterwards the club began rolling over its opponents week after week.

One team tried to keep the ball away from Joe with a

deliberate, ball-control offense. They had it for 34 of the 48 minutes and Joe still beat them, 25-0.

A.L. Williams remembers the state semi-finals that year very well. "We played Chalmette in one of the worst storms I've ever seen. The field was a mudhole and everyone was slipping and sliding all over the place. I still don't know how Joe got a handle on the ball, but he still passed beautifully. He threw for three touchdowns, though two of them were called back. But we won anyway, 14-0."

The next game gave Woodlawn a 14-0 record for the year and the only state title they've ever won. It was the end of a marvelous career for Joe at Woodlawn. The team was 34-4 in his three years at the helm, and his statistics were overwhelming.

As a senior, he set national passing records with 249 completions in 439 attempts for 3,290 yards. He had 40 touchdowns and completed 56.7 percent of his passes. For his career he had 439 completions in 931 attempts for 6,726 yards and 86 touchdowns. That is just an incredible achievement for a high school athlete playing in diehard football country.

It was an extremely happy time in Joe's life. When he thinks about the atmosphere at Woodlawn, the memories are warm and sentimental.

"Everything there seemed to revolve around the football team," he said. "It was one big community. Every morning I would look forward to getting into my sister's '64 Chevy to go to school. There was no pettiness, no jealousies. Everyone felt as if they were a part of something. It was just a great atmosphere to be in. For a young school we already had a great tradition."

So it was just about time for the latest local hero to move on. Bradshaw stayed near home and attended Louisiana Polytechnic Institute. Joe had recruiters coming to Woodlawn from all over the country. He still wasn't that big, standing 6'-1" and weighing about 180 pounds. But his arm and especially his quick release made a lot of schools very interested. Finally, he decided to attend the University of Arkansas in Fayetteville, and play his football in the tough southwest conference.

Joe arrived at Arkansas in the fall of 1969 and played with the freshman team that year. The Razorback varsity had a fine, 9-2, season, and were led by a junior quarterback named Bill Montgomery, who was an excellent passer. When Joe joined the varsity in 1970, Montgomery was the starting signal-caller and Joe the backup.

In the third game that year against Tulsa, Joe got his first taste of real action in the second half. He played extremely well, hitting on 11 of 15 passes for 144 yards as Arkansas won, 49-7. There was little doubt that the kid could move the ball through the air.

The Razorbacks had another fine team in 1970, and rolled over a number of their opponents. And with the big scores, Coach Frank Broyles was allowing his sophomore quarterback to see action. Against Baylor he threw his first college TD pass. Then he threw two more against an outclassed Wichita State team. These were long ones of 34 and 46 yards, as the Razorbacks won, 62-0. If anything happened to Montgomery, there was little doubt that Joe could do the job.

But Coach Broyles stayed with his senior most of the way and the team finished with another 9-2 record. When he was in there, Joe completed 48 of 86 passes for 744 yards and a fine, 55.8 completion percentage. He threw for four touchdowns and had five passes picked off. When Montgomery graduated and the 1971 season rolled around, the job was all Joe's.

In the season opener against California, Joe showed he was ready by hitting on 16 of 27 tosses for 228 yards and two scores. He was off and running on what was going to be an outstanding year.

Against Oklahoma State he hit on 22 of 35 and ran the ball in from 35 yards out for a score in a 31-10 victory. In the TCU game he completed 15 of 23 for 256 yards. Against Baylor he had TD tosses of 40 and 39 yards. In a big, 31-7, victory over archrival Texas, he passed for three scores and ran for another, hitting on 14 of 24 for 249 yards. He was named College Football Player of the Week. It was turning into a banner season for him.

Then came a strange game with Texas A&M. Joe threw all day, hitting 31 of 51 for 345 yards. Yet the Razorbacks managed just nine points and lost, 17-9. Joe was hurt in the SMU game and missed the regular season finale against Texas Tech. The Razorbacks were 8-2-1 on the regular season and second in the Southwest Conference. But they got a bid to the Liberty Bowl to play against Tennessee.

It was a close battle all the way. Tennessee took a 7-0 lead in the first period, but Joe got it back with a 36-yard scoring aerial to Jim Hodge in the second. His passes led to a pair of field goals in the second half, but Tennessee got the winning score late in the game after recovering an Arkansas fumble. The final was 14-13, but Joe was voted the Game's Outstanding Player after completing 18 of 28 passes for 200 yards.

As a junior he was outstanding, hitting on 160 of 271 passes for 2,203 yards, a 59.0 completion percentage, and 11 touchdowns. He scored another six times on the ground and had 12 passes picked off. His name began appearing on some All-America clubs, though not on the first team. Still, many thought by his senior year of 1972 he would have a chance to be the consensus All-American quarterback. It was also felt he might have a chance to make a run at the Heisman Trophy, given to the best college player in the land.

But there were problems from the outset. For one

thing, the Razorbacks were ranked number one in the country on some pre-season polls, so there was some added pressure right away. And a coaching change didn't help, either.

"We got a new offensive coach that year," Joe recalls, "and he changed the system we had been using since I got there."

It didn't help when the team lost its opener to powerful Southern California, 31-10. Joe played very well, hitting 19 of 37 passes for 223 yards, but the loss shook things up even more.

"After that loss, they began changing something every week, trying new plays and new formations. I started becoming confused," Joe said.

The team won its next two, but in the second of those, a 21-20 verdict over Tulsa, Joe completed just 10 of 23 for 75 yards. Not a typical Ferguson game, yet, he came back big the next week, firing 20 of 32 for 304 big yards and four touchdowns in a 27-13 win over TCU. When the team whipped Baylor, 31-20, for their fourth straight victory, it looked as if they were really back on the beam.

But then Texas derailed them, 35-15, as Joe had an erratic day with just 14 of 38 for 143 yards. The North Texas State game was easy, 42-16, with a more credible 15 of 21 for 256 yards. Then it started going sour. There was a 10-7 loss to Texas A&M and a last-minute 23-20 defeat by Rice. In that game Joe was three of 12 for 37 yards.

When the team lost to SMU, 22-7, the season was all but lost. In what would be his final game as a Razorback, Joe found himself on the bench. The team decided to try a wishbone type offense and they played a sophomore quarterback, Scott Bull. It was a disappointing finish to what had been a fine career.

"It was a bad year all around and I made some mistakes," Joe said. "Anyone who doesn't admit he makes them is crazy. To tell the truth, I was happy it ended, but then I began to worry about the draft and how the season would affect me."

A look at Joe's senior stats shows something was wrong. He completed just 119 of 254 passes for 1,484 yards and a 46.9 completion percentage. He had nine TD's and 15 intercepts. He had thrown the ball just 16 fewer times than his junior year, but gained some 700 yards less. His passing percentage also dropped some 12 points as the team fell to a 6-5 record.

A year earlier he was a projected first-round pick in the NFL draft. Now, he didn't know. Having made up his mind some time earlier that he wanted to play pro ball, it was inevitable that he would be chosen. He hoped it would turn into a good situation for him, a place where he could learn and play, and a team that would win.

Back home in Louisiana, he waited. The first round passed and no one had chosen Joe Ferguson. Then came the second round, and still none of the pros wanted the quarterback with the quick release. It could have been the problems he had during his senior year or the fact that the pros didn't feel he had enough size. After all, his predecessor at Woodlawn, Terry Bradshaw, had been the number one choice of the entire NFL when the Pittsburgh Steelers picked him three years earlier.

On the third round Joe was chosen by the Buffalo Bills, whose head coach, Lou Saban, said: "I was really surprised he lasted that long and was available. We would have taken him earlier, but we really felt it imperative to bolster our interior lines at the time. But we sure were happy to see him still there and decided not to wait any longer."

The Buffalo Bills. They were an old American Football League original, formed in 1960 when the new AFL began play. By 1964 the Bills were one of the powers in the new league, finishing with a 12-2 record and winning the AFL title with a win over the San Diego Chargers. They repeated the following year and were one of the few AFL teams that people thought could compete successfully with the older NFL teams at the time.

A year later, in 1966, they won another divisional title, finishing at 9-4-1. But that year they lost the championship game to the Kansas City Chiefs, depriving the Bills of a chance to play in the first Super Bowl game ever against the Green Bay Packers.

But afterwards, the club began to fade rapidly, as veterans declined and the young players weren't of the same quality. They dropped to 4-10 in 1967, then bottomed out at 1-12-1 the following year. The next three years were equally futile, and in 1971, when the club went an embarrassing 1-13, it was time to take action.

The two leagues had merged by then and the Bills were competing in an enlarged National Football League, being soundly beaten by old NFL teams as well as the former AFL ballclubs. It was frankly an embarrassing situation for a team once considered its league's best.

In 1972, Coach Lou Saban was brought in to rebuild the franchise. The team already had a potential superstar, running back O.J. Simpson, who had been the most talked about collegian of his time. O.J. came in 1969 and found himself running behind an offensive line nicknamed aptly, "the vanishing five." With no blocking whatsoever, the Juice became just another back, gaining 697, 488, and 742 yards his first three seasons respectively. And that was one reason Coach Saban wanted to rebuild his lines.

He was beginning to do that. In 1972 he picked up guard Reggie McKenzie, and a year later guard Joe De-Lameilleure and tackle Paul Seymour. But even in '72, there was improvement. The team finished at 4-9-1, but their philosophy was changing. Saban had restructured his offense around the Juice, and O.J. responded with 1,251 yards. He was still a great runner and Saban envisioned him doing much better in the future.

The incumbent quarterback at the time was Dennis Shaw, drafted out of San Diego State in 1970, where he was an outstanding collegiate passer. Shaw had a fine rookie year, but since then had not improved to the satisfaction of the coaching staff. He was too inconsistent. A pair of fine wide receivers had joined the club in 1971, J.D. Hill and Bob Chandler, but Shaw was still throwing too many interceptions. Coach Saban wanted a more controlled quarterback, especially if the offense was going to be built around a ground attack. That's why he took Joe Ferguson in 1973.

Joe was happy with the selection and added, "I didn't even know where Buffalo was! I had heard rumors that I might be going to Dallas where I probably wouldn't play much but would certainly learn a lot about winning. But when I saw the Bills' brochure and realized they were such a young team, it was encouraging and gave me a new kind of feeling."

Being from Louisiana, Joe was not at all thrilled when he heard stories of the bitterly frigid, snow-filled Buffalo winters. Figuring he couldn't have everything the way he wanted it, he still was very excited about reporting and beginning his pro career. But, his knowledge of the pro game was pretty limited.

"I really didn't pay much attention to pro football then," he said. "The only time I watched it on TV was the Monday night games, and my only real interest was in Terry Bradshaw because we grew up together in Shreveport and were old friends. I never even watched much as a kid, in fact, because I would always rather be out doing something than just watching."

But before Joe was to report to his first training camp,

he received a surprise. Coach John McKay of USC, surprised everyone by naming two Louisiana products, Bert Jones, headed for the Colts, and Joe Ferguson to play the college All-Star game. Joe didn't think he'd be named and the experience did not turn out to be a good one.

"The selection was a mixed-emotions kind of thing with me," Joe said. "I have to admit I was honored being picked. But at the same time it cost me three weeks of valuable training time with the Bills, and for a rookie that's every important. Then it became particularly annoying when I barely played in the game against Miami. Bert saw most of the action."

When he finally reached camp, he had to learn all the plays, the system, meet his teammates, and learn the particular traits of the other players on the offensive unit. It's a lot to take in, especially in the first year.

Because he arrived so late, Joe didn't play in the first two preseason games. The Bills lost both of them, but it was already obvious that they were trying to build a powerful running attack around O.J. The offensive line was much improved and geared for the run. The fullback was a 250-lb. bruiser named Jim Braxton, who could provide additional blocking for "the Juice."

Finally, Coach Saban decided to start his rookie in the third preseason game against the Washington Redskins. But it wasn't just an ordinary game. It marked the team's first appearance ever in its brand new stadium in Orchard Park, New York, outside Buffalo. A sellout crowd of 80,020 fans was there to see the Bills and the new facility. For a kid from Louisiana this must have been quite a sight.

But Joe kept his cool. The Skins had a fine team in 1973 and they did a job on the Buffalo defense, winning the game, 37-21. But the fans might have found a new hero. All three Buffalo touchdowns came as a result of

Joe Ferguson passes. He played with poise and intelligence, stood up well under the Washington pass-rush, and still showed that quick release and accuracy that had marked his entire football career.

Though he played sporadically in spots after that, often making the usual rookie mistakes, he showed enough to impress the right people. The Bills failed to win a game in the pre-season, losing six straight, and that might be another reason the coaches decided to gamble. Rookie Joe Ferguson was named the Bills' starting quarterback for the regular season opener against the New England Patriots.

"I didn't get a whole lot of sleep the night before that one," Joe remembers. "I got to bed early enough, but I kept thinking about the plays we'd be using and how I would execute them. And I couldn't help wondering how I would play. What would happen, for instance, if I stunk out the stadium?"

That didn't exactly happen. In fact, Joe was at the helm early in the game when the Bills moved to a 7-6 lead. He was hit hard and shaken up. Dazed, he had to leave the game and Dennis Shaw took over, completing what turned out to be a surprise, 31-13, victory.

It probably didn't matter who was at quarterback that day, for it was all O.J. He ran all over the Patriots and was virtually unstoppable every time he touched the ball. When the game had ended, Simpson had carried 29 times and had set a new NFL record at the time of 250 yards.

It seemed to set the tone for the season. Joe was back at the helm a week later as the club lost to San Diego. But then came victories over the New York Jets, Philadelphia Eagles, and Baltimore Colts. Suddenly, the perennial losers, the Bills, were at 4-1 and challenging for the division lead!

The man of the hour was Simpson, who was finally

running wild as had been expected since 1969. There was even talk of the Juice challenging Jim Brown's long-standing record of 1,863 yards in a season. The tremendous publicity generated by O.J. and the team's success was actually helpful to Joe.

"With O.J. carrying so much and getting so many yards, the pressure was kind of off me," Joe recalls. "The whole system that year gave me more of a chance to look at the defenses and learn. They were playing zones by then, and I didn't really have to throw at them too often."

The rookie was also getting the plays from Saban on the sideline, another move to take pressure off him. And he was doing the job, though he was throwing less than any other starting quarterback in the league. That made it difficult to get a real feel for the passing game. The team often went to the pass in tough situations, like third-and-long. So Joe's percentage was not good, but it wasn't a true reflection of his skills.

Fortunately, Joe was getting along very well with Dennis Shaw, the man he replaced.

"Dennis is a very calm guy and he helped me all he could," Joe remembers. "He doesn't worry about things on or off the field and maybe that's why he took my replacing him so well. But when the defense was in and I was on the sidelines, Dennis would stand with me and remind me what to look for in the opposing defenses."

The team continued to play well, though they did not have the talent or the depth of the really top teams. But with O.J. running to daylight against everyone, they had the potential to beat any team. What hurt them most was a three-game losing streak at midseason. They went in at 5-2, and came out at 5-5, losing to New Orleans, Cincinnati, and Miami. Still, Joe was optimistic about his team and its future.

"There's a real good atmosphere here," he said.

"We're a young team and also a very determined one. In each game you can see the kind of potential that's here. What we need is more consistency and I think it will come, maybe not this year or even next year. But we have quality players and coaches, and we're going to be a good football team. We've got the desire to win and eventually we will."

But there was still more winning to be done in '73. The club beat Baltimore again, then Atlanta. And in the final two games against New England and the Jets, O.J. Simpson took center stage as no athlete had done in a long time.

Against the Patriots he was unstoppable again. He rolled for 216 yards, leaving him with 1,803 yards, just 60 short of Jim Brown's record. The Bills won the game, 37-13, and now the whole football world was watching as the Juice would be going after the record in the team's final game against the Jets.

It was played in New York and the snow was falling, the field partially frozen and slippery. Joe was the quarterback and both he and the rest of the offense wanted to get Juice the record fast. Joe continued to feed the ball to his running back, O.J. broke the record before the first quarter had ended. But then there were two more immediate objectives, win the game and see if the Juice could go over the mythical 2,000-yard mark.

For the remainder of the game the Bills pounded at the Jets, and Simpson carried the ball. When it ended, the team had a 34-14 victory and O.J. Simpson had carried 34 times for 200 more yards and 2,003 for the season!

It was an almost storybook season for the Bills. Besides Simpson's incredible and successful run at Jim Brown's rushing record, the team had surprised everyone. Coming off a 4-9-1 season in 1972, the Bills finished the '73 campaign with a 9-5 mark, good for second place in the AFC Eastern Division behind Miami. They missed a wildcard playoff berth by the margin of a single game.

As for the rookie quarterback, it had to be a successful year, in view of the accomplishments of the team. Joe's own stats showed just 73 completions in 164 passes for 939 yards and a 44.5 completion percentage. He threw for four touchdowns and had 10 picked off. In addition, he ran the ball 48 times and gained another 147 yards. The passing stats would have undoubtedly been better if the Bills were not such a rush-oriented team. But there were few complaints about the job Joe had done under the circumstances.

The team had to continue building. The 1974 draft brought tight end Reuben Gant on the first round, then, surprisingly, a quarterback on the second. He was Gary Marangi of Boston College. But Joe was still considered the main man. The team had traded Dennis Shaw to St. Louis, so they needed a new back-up man. The coaches felt there would also have to be some additional changes if the club was going to be a bona fide playoff contender.

"We knew right away that we'd have to throw more in '74, said Coach Saban. "O.J. and our running attack kind of caught everyone by surprise last year. It was a special kind of thing, but NFL teams are too good to let it happen again. But we liked what we saw in Joe and he kept improving right up to the end of the year. We felt he could do the job."

He looked good in training camp prior to the season, which lead wide receiver Bob Chandler to comment, "I've never seen such quick development in a quarterback."

But Joe had always been a fast learner, and he'd need to be sharp in the opening game when the club went up against the aggressive, always tough Oakland Raiders.

The game would be played on a Monday night, with a national television audience. The game was in Buffalo and full house of 80,020 fans were in attendance.

It was a close defensive struggle for most of the first half. Then, with less than a minute remaining in the second period, O.J. got the football, was hit hard, and limped off the field with a twisted ankle. It was at half-time the team learned he wouldn't be returning in the second half.

"It was a strange feeling without O.J.," Joe recalls. "A lot of the guys were just looking at each other and thinking, 'Oh, Lord.' "

In the third period the Oakland defense attempted to intimidate Joe, but he stood in there against their aggressive pass rush. In the fourth period he showed his poise under pressure. Twice, in the closing minutes of action he brought the Bills from behind with pinpoint passing. Each time he culminated drives with touchdowns passes to wide receiver Ahmad Rashad, who had come over in the Dennis Shaw trade. Joe and his teammates held their breaths as Oakland's grand old man, George Blanda, barely missed a long field goal as time ran out. Buffalo had won the game, 21-20, and Joe Ferguson was the man of the hour.

"The game really gave me a boost," Joe said, afterward. "It was a great feeling to know we could do it against a good team without O.J. I try to be a realist about things. I know I'm not the greatest passer in the world. I'm not as strong as a Joe Namath or Terry Bradshaw, but I know I can be the quarterback of a winning team."

Joe was showing characteristic modesty. His teammates didn't necessarily agree. They felt they had quite a young passer in their midst.

"I was pleasantly surprised by the way Joe performed," said O.J., whose injury was not serious.

"He's come on better than anyone expected. Now when you play the Bills, it's not just playing O.J. You have to stop Joe Ferguson, as well."

And Ahmad Rashad, still one of the better receivers in the league, said at the time. "Joe throws plenty hard, but the thing I noticed most is that he is able to put the ball into the tight spots so well."

O.J. returned the next week but the team lost to tough Miami, 24-16. Afterwards they went on a big, six-game winning streak, whipping the Jets, the Packers, the Colts, the Bears, and the New England Patriots twice. Though Joe was throwing more than he had the previous year, the Bills were still mainly a running team and he wasn't putting it up nearly as often as many of the other signal-callers in the league. But with the team winning, he was certainly enjoying himself. Yet at the same time he was feeling certain kinds of pressure, which he freely talked about as well.

"It's been a good year, so far," he said. "I really enjoyed the two games we had against New England (The Bills had won, 30-28, and 29-28 in a couple of real barnburners.) I enjoyed the pressure and I would say that even if we had lost.

"Strangely enough, in some ways I find more pressure on me from the people back home. The way they feel about football and I guess with the success Terry is having now at Pittsburgh, they also expect a lot from me. I sometimes find myself wondering what they would think if I suddenly decided to retire. They have high hopes for me, but in some ways it's not right for them to be that way."

That was a kind of strange statement. Perhaps Joe was hearing from many of his former fans from Woodlawn and their own goals for him exceeded his early accomplishments. It's hard to say, but he was obviously feeling a strange kind of pressure from the home country that he wasn't getting in Buffalo or from his teammates. He admitted he had given some thought to the drafting of Gary Marangi and felt he would soon face a personal challenge from the strong-armed youngster.

"I realize we're two young guys in the same place at the same time," he said. "But I can't worry about what may happen down the road. If I'm not doing the job I'll know it and get out."

With the Bills riding high with a 7-1 mark and a serious contender for the AFC East title, there was naturally talk about the playoffs and a possible run at the Super Bowl. In most cases, teams with young quarterbacks just do not get that far under playoff pressure.

"If we get that far I think I can do it," Joe said. "If I were looking at another quarterback under similar circumstances, I would probably have doubts, too. Young guys don't usually do much, but then again they aren't generally in those kinds of situations."

So there were a lot of different kinds of pressures working from within and also from the outside. Joe continued to handle them all well. Looking back now, it seemed obvious that after eight games, with a 7-1 mark, the Bills were playing a bit over their heads. There just weren't that many outstanding players, and in the last six games, some of these weaknesses began showing through. In addition, O.J., while having another fine year, was not gobbling up the yards in the same fashion as he had the season before.

The win streak came to an end with a 21-9 loss to Houston, followed by a tough, 35-28 defeat by Miami. Wins over Cleveland and Baltimore followed, putting the team back in a tie for first with Miami at 9-3. But the club then lost its final two games, to the Jets and L.A. Rams. That brought them to a second straight 9-5 finish, but was good enough to earn the Bills a wildcard game in the playoffs.

Simpson had another fine year with 1,125 yards, and Rashad was the leading receiver with just 36 catches for 433 yards. Joe finished with 119 completions in 232 attempts for 1,588 yards and a 51.3 percentage, 12 touchdowns and 12 intercepts. They were good stats, not great, but then again they reflect on the actual lack of throwing. Playing in all 14 games in both of his first two years, he averaged just 11.7 passes his first year and 16.6 his second season. In the high-powered game of the '70s, that wasn't much at all.

But now there was a playoff game to contend with, and the Bills would not have it easy. They would be going up against the Pittsburgh Steelers, and that meant that Joe would be playing head to head against his old Shreveport buddy, Terry Bradshaw. In the eyes of most, the Steelers were a much deeper and more powerful team than the Bills, and they were heavy favorites.

Both Ferguson and Bradshaw wished each other well. Their sentiments were similar. Each said he hoped the other played well.

The first quarter was fairly even. The Steelers scored first on a 21-yard field goal by Roy Gerela. Later in the period Joe got the Bills moving. The Steelers were containing Simpson pretty well, but Joe hit on several key passes, finally bringing the ball down to the Pittsburgh 22. From there, he faded back, spotted tight end Paul Seymour, and hit the receiver in the end zone for a score. John Leypoldt's kick made it a 7-3 game, and Bills' fans had hope.

But in the second period it all came apart. The Steeler offensive machine suddenly exploded. First, Bradshaw hit Rocky Bleier with a 27-yard TD toss. Then on each of the next three possessions, the Steelers drove quickly downfield and each time fullback Franco Harris went over from inside the five. By the time the period had ended Pittsburgh scored four times, and although two of the extra point tries were blocked. Pittsburgh took an insurmountable 29-7 lead into the locker room at half-time. Bradshaw had been brilliant, completing seven of eight passes for 143 yards in the second period alone.

So the final sessions were desperation time. The Bills were forced out of their game plan and couldn't really get anything going. Pittsburgh coasted to a 32-14 victory on their way to what would eventually be four Super Bowl triumphs in the next six years. So the Bills had been clearly beaten by the best and had nothing to be ashamed about. It was nevertheless a very successful season.

On the surface, the team was still strengthening itself, so there were high hopes for 1975. And while O.J. had another banner year with more than 1,800 yards, the team showed an alarming tendency toward backsliding, especially on defense. Though they finished at 8-6, still a winning record, the club was just 4-6 after winning their first four, including a 30-21 triumph over Pittsburgh.

The biggest problem seemed to be with the defense. In the second half of the season the Bills lost games by scores of 35-30, 42-35, 33-24, 31-21, and 35-13. They also won by a couple of big scores, 45-31, and 24-23. No team is going to be a serious contender if it gives up 355 points in 14 games.

One of the few bright spots all year was the play of Joe Ferguson. With so many high-scoring games, Joe had to open it up more and he did. He wound up with 169 completions in 321 attempts for 2,426 yards and an improved, 52.6 percentage. But the most impressive thing was his team record 25 touchdown passes, as opposed to just 17 interceptions. He also set another Buffalo mark by throwing at least one scoring pass in 12 straight games. There seemed little doubt that Joe continued to be the Buffalo quarterback of the future.

There were people, as mentioned, who wondered in

just what direction the team would go in 1976. Some thought the club might be just a .500 team again, but no one could have been prepared for what happened. The team lost its first two to Miami and Houston, then won a pair, over Tampa Bay and Kansas City. They were 2-2 and still optimistic. They shouldn't have been. The Bills simply would not win another game all year. They would lose 10 in a row and fall to the bottom of the division with a 2-12 mark, an incredible turnaround.

That wasn't all. Midway through the season Joe suffered the first serious injury of his career. He broke four transverse processes in his lower back. It was a painful injury and he had to miss the final seven games. Also, after the sixth game Lou Saban had been replaced by Jim Ringo. So the team was really in disarray.

For his abbreviated season, Joe had completed just 74 of 151 passes for 1,086 yards and nine touchdowns. He completed but 49 percent of his passes. But the amazing thing was in spite of the team record and often having to play catchup, he threw just a single interception until his injury. It was a league record for fewest intercepts in a season and the lowest interception percentage.

Yet all was not going well now. Simpson was still there and had gained another 1,503 yards in '76 despite the awful record. But there were many question marks. Marangi had had his shot and was also gone. The new backup QB was Fred Basana from California.

Joe felt he was playing some of the best ball of his career before his injury in '76. But things turned sour in a hurry the next year. The club lost six of its first seven games and was destined for another horrible season, this one at 3-11, and Joe Ferguson remembers it as one of the most frustrating of his life.

"I liked Jim Ringo," Joe said. "It was tough for both of us to watch what was happening to the team. The running game wasn't doing well, even before O.J. hurt his knee. Then, it was nothing. It's hard to say where the problems were, but there were also a lot of internal problems upstairs."

There were also orders to open up the passing attack which were said to have come from the front office. The result was that Joe threw more than ever, hitting 221 of 457 for 2,803 yards and 12 scores. But the general disorganization in the offense resulted in just a 48.4 percentage and 24 intercepts. And there was plenty of booing. Not one to point a finger, Joe said another problem in '77 involved the great O.J., who apparently was beginning to complain publically that he was tired of losing.

"I think O.J. really hurt himself with the players when he started to complain," Joe said. "He got a lot of people off him because of that, especially within the team. I like O.J. a lot. He's done a great deal for the Bills and helped me as well, but I think the team will be better off without him.

"It's bad enough losing without having one of your own teammates come out and say that the team isn't going anywhere and the coaching staff isn't doing the job, things like that. I don't know, maybe he thought that was his way to help the team since he could say more than the rest of us. Maybe he figured by going public he could put pressure on management to make changes. Then again, maybe he was just trying to get out of there."

Joe's comments came after the season when O.J. was out. He was traded to San Francisco so he could finish his career in his native California. But he was never the same runner again.

Rebuilding. That can be a frightening word for a football player who wants to win. It means the team isn't going to win now and is looking for the future. But rebuilding is what the Bills had to do. They picked up a running back they hoped would replace O.J., Terry

Miller of Oklahoma State, and got a fine veteran wide receiver, Frank Lewis, from Pittsburgh. They also tried to shore up the defense with new players.

Joe, of course, would be back for his sixth year at quarterback. In the eyes of many knowledgeable football people, he was not getting his due. They considered him one of the better young signal-callers in the league. But the Buffalo system was not conducive to bringing out the best in him. Now that the team was changing, maybe it would be. He deserved a chance to really run a team the way the top QB's of the period were doing. Players like Bradshaw, Dan Fouts, Bob Griese, Ken Stabler, Jim Zorn, Roger Staubach, Archie Manning were all getting the chance to run balanced attacks, which featured a lot of wide-open passing, the direction in which the game seemed to be going.

There was another change prior to the 1978 season that had everyone excited. The team had another new coach, but this one had the oustanding track record. He was Chuck Knox, who had just spent five years coaching the L.A. Rams to five straight divisional titles. In that time his record was 44-15-1. He was a winner, a good handler of personnel, and a motivator. He didn't promise to win overnight, but he indicated it wouldn't be that long until he had the kind of team he wanted on the shores of Lake Erie.

One thing Knox didn't question was his starting quarterback. It would be Joe Ferguson all the way. The backup would be aging veteran Bill Munson, an experienced and smooth player, but a guy who wouldn't be capable of handling the whole load anymore. He'd be the perfect backup for Joe and Ferguson agreed.

"Bill is so calm and relaxed. I just look at him and say, 'Here's a guy who has been around.' He knows how to accept things without getting upset. He's been there before and he's been on the bottom before and he knows how to handle it.''

Joe had also settled into a comfortable lifestyle in the Buffalo area by this time, though it was so low key that not too many people really knew much about him. He still longed for Louisiana and made his permanent home in Natchitoches, which is about 60 miles south of Shreveport. He was also becoming, at this time, more outspoken about the things going on around him.

He lived in an apartment complex near the Stadium in Orchard Park and rarely went into the main part of the city. In 1977 he shared a house with backup Fred Basana and was very upset when Basana was cut before 1978. Many of his other friends were outside of football, some of them connected with horses. On off days he often went to the nearby town of Boston, New York, where he tended the horses and went riding at the farm of a friend.

"I've been lucky," he said, "because I've met some people up here who mean a lot to me. They're good friends and I can go out with them, sit and talk, and not think about football or have them thinking about football.''

Back home in the off-season he got involved with raising Arabian horses, and he called those he owned "a source of pride and relaxation." He also has a private pilot's license and owns his own airplane. He also did some volunteer coaching at Northwestern Louisiana State College, where he works with the quarterbacks, throws with them, and lifts weights to stay in condition and keep sharp.

He remained a very private person, never making any of the bar or singles scenes in the Buffalo area. Even back home he lives a basically quiet and unpretentious life, not always the norm for an admired star athlete.

But as his good friend, Bert Jones, has said:

"I don't think the genuineness of Joe will ever leave him. That's the reason he's a good friend of mine and always has been. He's just the same ol' Joe."

Jones also respected Joe as a fellow quarterback and said things about him that not too many people ever mentioned because of the Buffalo situation.

"As far as I'm concerned, Joe's the best natural thrower in the NFL. Our coach, Ted Marchibroda, respects him as much as, if not more than any quarterback we play against."

Part of Joe's problem in getting the respect that by now was really due him was his relationship with the press. It hadn't always been the best because of the quickness to criticize and seek controversy.

"Sometimes I find the press rather depressing," he said. "They're strange. You read the articles regularly and one week you're a hero and the next you're a dog. Sometimes I just can't understand how a guy can see so much good one week and then turn around and see so much bad the next. Now I don't even read the stuff, especially if I think it's negative. That doesn't do me any good."

Over the years there were various types of charges, one of the big ones being that Joe was not a take-charge type leader, like his good friend, Bert Jones. To this, Joe answered:

"I know. I've seen Bert on television running up and down the field and hollering all kinds of stuff. But that's not me. I've got to play my way. The only way I've ever been able to lead is to do the job. If I do what's right both on and off the field, I feel that's a legitimate way of leading. As much as I like Bert, and he may be my best friend in the world, I can't be like him when it comes to that."

So Joe was doing it his way. And Chuck Knox didn't

hesitate in making his commitment to Joe as his quarterback. For the first time in several years Joe had a real good feeling. He wasn't expecting the Bills to turn it around in one year, but he admitted the past couple of seasons after those early years of promise, were particularly tough to take.

"A couple of times I wanted to pack my bags and leave without telling anyone I was going," Joe said. "But then your inner self says, 'Don't quit!' If you're a competitor, you don't want to quit. You just reach a point where you start thinking of yourself and doing your job without worrying about anyone else."

Joe said his feeling was that the team collapsed from the top down, until the hiring of Chuck Knox.

"We lost players without getting anything in return, we changed head coaches twice, and the fans went crazy. And it seemed as if management didn't care. It was a total collapse."

The 1978 season was pretty much a year of transition. The offense seemed to come around before the defense, so there were once again a number of high scoring games. It was also the first year of the sixteen-game schedule, so the clubs all had to get used to the two extra games.

The Bills opened with a loss to the Steelers, 28-17, then dropped a pair of close ones, 21-20, to the Jets, and 31-24 to the Dolphins. Then victories over Baltimore and Kansas City followed. Joe was playing very well. Knox was trying to reestablish his running game, so he didn't have his quarterback throwing all that much. In the Kansas City game, Joe had completed 15 of 18 passes and after the fifth week of the season was the top rated passer in the league.

But the team continued to lose more than it won. The only other victories all year were against Cincinnati, the New York Giants, and the Colts in the final game. The club checked in at 5-11 in the first year under Knox, yet it was a promising 5-11. Most of the players felt the team was on the way up, not down.

As for Joe, he had a good, but not great year, completing 175 of 330 passes for 2,136 yards, a 53.0 percentage, 16 touchdowns and 15 intercepts. It was a solid year. The running game also seemed to revive with Terry Miller gaining 1,060 yards. So everyone looked to '79 as the year the team might begin making a move.

Coach Knox added a host of new players as he began to change the complexion of the team for 1979. Some important additions were explosive wide receiver Jerry Butler, safety Jeff Nixon, and veteran linebacker Isiah Robertson, acquired in a trade with L.A. Young Dan Manucci was drafted out of Kansas State to back up Joe at quarterback.

Joe was also excited about the new season. His performance had tailed off somewhat in the second half of the '78 season, and he wound up the tenth rated passer in the league. There were once again a few calls for a change at that crucial position. But the coach repeatedly told the press and anyone else who asked that he felt the team could and would win with Ferguson at the signal-calling spot.

The opening game of '79 was a heartbreaker as the Bills lost a squeaker to the Dolphins, 9-7, as kicker Tom Dempsey missed a 34-yard field goal that could have won it on the last play of the game. It was a quiet debut for Joe, who threw just 13 times and completed seven for 76 yards. Add to that the fact that the Bills' runners gained just 45, and you have a pretty dismal offensive showing.

But what a difference a week can make. The following Sunday, hosting the Cincinnati Bengals, the team exploded for the second highest point total in the history of the franchise. They whipped the Bengals, 51-24, as

Joe passed for 282 yards, Roland Hooks ran for four touchdowns, and rookie Jerry Butler caught seven passes for 116 yards. So for the first two weeks of the season the Bills were a Jekyll-Hyde outfit. But they definitely had the capabilities of coming up big on offense.

A 27-19 loss to San Diego followed with the Chargers bottling up the Buffalo running game. But Joe still passed for 257 yards and a pair of touchdowns, and was off to a very fast start for the second year in a row. When the team returned to Orchard Park the following week to meet the New York Jets, they exploded again.

The game started quietly enough, the Bills taking a 6-3 lead at the end of one. In the second period the Jets got two quick scores by running back Tom Newton to go ahead, 17-6. The Bills got one back on a Ferguson to Butler pass from the five, though the point was blocked, but then the Jets Richard Todd hit Wesley Walker from 37 yards out, New York had a 24-12 lead.

Then came a big play. The Bills had the ball at their own eight-yard line with just 24 seconds left in the half. Joe promptly threw to Terry Miller for seventeen yards and a first down at the 25. Then, with time running out, he dropped back again and threw a long, high pass for Frank Lewis. The ball was tapped by defensive back Burgess Owens and bounced in the air. Suddenly the flashing form of Jerry Butler took the ball on the dead run and the rookie ran it all the way to the end zone for a 75-yard TD pass. The kick made it 24-19, Jets, at the half.

The "Big Ben" pass (it was a play they had practiced) gave the Bills a real boost. They came back out on fire. Early in the third period there was Butler again, taking a 74-yard TD toss from Ferguson. Then, minutes later, the rookie caught a nine-yarder from Joe for the score. A recovered fumble gave the Bills still another touchdown and they rolled to a 46-31 victory.

Rookie Butler broke an NFL record by catching ten passes for 255 yards and four scores. Joe hit on 19 of 30 passes for 367 yards and five touchdowns. It was the biggest day of his career.

A week later against the Colts, Joe completed 14 of 23 passes for another 317 yards and three more scores, as the Bills won again 31-13, raising their record to 3-2. It was Joe's second straight 300-yard game, and he also became the first Bills' quarterback to pass for more than 250 yards in four straight games during the same season. He was also the hottest quarterback in the NFL.

Asked to comment on Joe's performance, his good friend and rival quarterback, Bert Jones, said:

"Joe's finally getting more help. He's always been one of the best throwers I've ever seen. The team is just a little more well-rounded and it's making Joe a more effective quarterback."

Coach Knox was also more than pleased with his QB. "Joe is doing as good a job as any of the quarterbacks I've had," the coach said. "And I've been with a lot of super quarterbacks, like Joe Namath, Ron Jaworski, John Hadl, and Pat Haden."

And Joe himself said he was getting more confidence in himself and in the team. He wasn't letting things bother him and was getting a great deal of help from veteran Munson. He was also quite realistic about the '79 version of the Bills.

"We're shooting for a .500 season," he said. "If we win ten games we'll be elated. We're still not a great team like the Steelers or Cowboys, but we're good. We're a team of the future and that's what we're building for."

There was a letdown the next week, a 7-0 loss to Chicago. But the game was played on a rainy afternoon and neither team could mount any kind of passing attack. The difference was Chicago great Walter Payton, who ran for 155 yards and scored the only TD. Joe completed just five of 21 passes for 50 yards, yet after six weeks of the season, he was the leading passer in the entire NFL.

In six games he had completed 77 of 137 passes for 1,358 yards and ten scores. When asked to talk about his season and career to this point, Joe was again very candid.

"I don't think I've been a bad quarterback," he said. "I don't think I've ever played badly enough to be considered the worst quarterback in the league. But by the same token, I haven't had the great, great, great season that some people have had.

"But the last three weeks I've felt more comfortable and more relaxed. I'm feeling that I've been accomplishing something in the NFL. And now, when you're talking about the top quarterbacks in the league —Jones, Bradshaw, Griese—I think you would have to say I fit in there with them.

"My whole attitude has changed. I don't worry about the mistakes I make like I used to. And I don't let the mistakes bother me."

Realistically, it was going to be a season of ups and downs, and Joe knew it. The running game was disappearing quickly and Joe couldn't do it alone. The team lost to the Dolphins, 17-7, then to the Colts in a rematch, 14-13. Joe threw for over 200 yards again, and after the game a Buffalo newsman put it this way.

"What stands between the Buffalo Bills and outright disaster is quarterback Joe Ferguson. His freshly blossomed maturity apparently was not a temporary state. Sunday, against Baltimore, he repeatedly made the best of bad situations, coolly stepping out of trouble and scanning the field for open receivers. That produced one touchdown and should have produced another, but it was nullified by a penalty."

Joe wasn't always the writers' best friend, but he was gaining new-found respect all over the league. The club split its next two after Baltimore, then won three straight, bringing its record to 7-6. They still had a good chance for a .500 year.

Next came Denver. And while the Broncos won it, 19-16, Joe completed 27 of 46 passes for 313 yards. It was the fourth time he was over the 300-yard mark and it enabled him to become the first Buffalo quarterback to go over 3,000 yards in a season. He was also calling his own plays for the first time, as Coach Knox felt it would eventually give him more leadership abilities on the field.

Unfortunately, the team lost its final two games to put a damper on what had been a satisfying rebuilding season. They finished at 7-9, but with high hopes for the future. And for Joe Ferguson, it was his greatest season as a pro.

Joe completed 238 of 458 passes for 3,572 yards and a 52.0 percentage. He threw for 14 TD's and had 15 intercepted. His average gain per pass of 7.80 was one of the best in the league. There was no doubt about it, he had come of age.

Before 1980, Coach Knox again added a group of new players, mixing youngsters and veterans. For instance, he drafted an elusive running back out of Auburn, Joe Cribbs, in an attempt to solidify the ground attack, which disappeared the second half of 1979. He traded for veteran linebacker Phil Villapiano and an experienced short-yardage fullback in Roosevelt Leaks. Plus a group of other young players stuck. The coach was trying to strike that delicate balance that often means the difference between a good and a great season.

Joe was now going into his eighth season in the league. He had seen both the good and the bad side of being a pro signal-caller, but he still had goals and aspirations, things he wanted to achieve.

"My goal since I've been here has been to get in the Pro Bowl and the Super Bowl," he said. "I was close to the Pro Bowl last year, but playing in the AFC you're going against some stud quarterbacks."

Then Joe talked about the three other NFL quarterbacks from his home state of Louisiana, and he made some interesting comparisons.

"If you mold a quarterback, you'd mold Terry Bradshaw," Joe said. "He's strong, has good size, a tremendous arm, and can run.

"Bert Jones has a tremendous arm, can run, and is courageous. He fears no one. And he's very intelligent. That may be his only asset over Terry—though Terry is a heady player.

"Doug Williams (the young Tampa Bay QB, also from Louisiana) has a tremendous arm. He just needs experience. He needs time, like Bert, Terry, and I needed.

"As for myself, I think I'm as good as anyone. I wish I had the size of those guys. But I think we all have qualities to be top-notch quarterbacks."

So Joe had the confidence to rank himself with the best. Now, with the 1980 season about to begin, he was determined to go out and prove it. The team had put in some new wrinkles. One of them was for Joe, a shotgun formation, similar to the one the Dallas Cowboys have used successfully for years. The quarterback in the shotgun takes a direct snap some seven yards deep and doesn't have to drop back. It's a passing formation generally used on third down plays. Joe liked it.

"It's easier to read the defense from the shotgun because you're standing up instead of crouching over the center. And since you don't have to drop back, the offensive linemen know where you are, so it's easier for them to block. It makes our passing game more versatile, so I think I'm going to like it."

By the time the opener came around the Bills were very satisfied. Rookie runner Cribbs looked like a real find, and the defense seemed much improved. This was the team Knox had built and he expected them to win.

The opener against Miami was a big one in many ways. For starters, the Bills had lost twenty consecutive games to the Dolphins. And for three periods it looked as if they'd lose another. They were trailing, 7-3, and Joe had already thrown five—yes, five—interceptions.

But he hung in there, driving the team downfield late in the game. The big play was a 29-yard pass to Butler, bringing the ball to the 11 with 3:56 left. Two plays later Joe passed to Roosevelt Leaks for the go-ahead score. A last-second touchdown following an interception made it a 17-7 finale. Joe wound up 20 of 32 for 198 yards despite the five intercepts, and rookie Cribbs lived up to his advance notices with 60 yards rushing and nine catches for 71 more. But as one newspaper put it:

"Ferguson's resilience was the key to the game. Three of four years ago he probably wouldn't have been able to bounce back with a strong fourth quarter under similar circumstances."

A fine beginning. Now the trick was to sustain it. Next came the potentially explosive New York Jets. Joe had another fine game with 18 of 29 for 207 yards and the defense excelled. Safety Jeff Nixon's 50-yard return of an interception iced the game as the Bills won, 20-10, jumping atop the AFC East with a 2-0 mark. There was a certain feeling in the air.

The next one was important to Joe. The Bills would be playing at the New Orleans Superdome against the Saints. It would be his first game in his home state since his rookie year of 1973. It turned into a wide-open game. The Saints actually had a 19-14 halftime lead. But in the third period Joe hit Frank Lewis for an 18-yard score, and in the fourth he threw another one and Cribbs scored on the ground. The final was 35-26.

Joe had a 22 of 31 day for 295 yards. Butler caught five passes for 133 yards, Lewis six for 82, and rookie Cribbs ran for 89 yards and caught six passes for 52 more. The offense was really rolling. Plus the shotgun formation was helping the air attack.

"Being 3-0 is really a strange feeling," Joe said. "You don't get it too often in Buffalo. But it's a feeling that everything is coming together and everyone is helping each other out."

There was another significance to the New Orleans victory. Joe's passing yardage enabled him to surpass Jack Kemp as the all-time Buffalo passing leader. Kemp, now a representative in Congress, had 15,128 yards for the Bills between 1962 and 1969. Joe had now thrown for more yardage.

The next game showed just how far the Bills had come. They were up against the very tough Oakland Raiders and they dominated. The offense kept the ball for more than 41 minutes, while the Raiders had it for less than nineteen minutes. The final was 24-7, as Joe stuck with his short game and hit on 17 of 25 for 175 yards. Included was a pretty, 21-yard TD toss to Cribbs after faking a reverse. The Bills were now 4-0 and leading the AFC East and Joe was completing some 67 percent of his passes.

Next came the high-powered passing offense of the San Diego Chargers, which featured Dan Fouts throwing to the likes of John Jefferson, Charlie Joiner, and Kellen Winslow. This one proved that the Bills had learned how to win.

Trailing 24-12 in the final period, and not really having a big day offensively, Buffalo drove in twice, the first time Joe hit tight end Mark Brammer from the nine, and the second time Cribbs took it in from the three. Although Joe was just 14 of 28 for 129 yards, the Bills still won their fifth straight over one of the teams thought to be a possible Super Bowl winner. The final was 26-24, and people were beginning to wonder just how good a team Chuck Knox had built.

The next week the bubble burst for the first time. Playing against the Baltimore Colts and Joe's good buddy Bert Jones, the Bills were beaten, 17-12. Joe threw for 210 yards, Jones for 206, but the Colts put more points up. Buffalo was now tied with New England at 5-1, with the Colts at 4-2, in what was shaping up as a tight divisional race.

When three Joe Cribbs fumbles helped Miami defeat the Bills, 17-14, the following week, some thought perhaps the early wins were again false hopes. Joe hit on 24 of 42 for 221 yards, but he wasn't putting enough points on the board. A scoreless first two periods for the Bills put them in the hole, 14-0, and they had to play from behind. There was no respite in the schedule. The next week they would have a showdown game with New England, which now led them by a game.

With a 40-mile an hour wind blowing through the cold at Rich Stadium, the Bills came home and proved once and for all that they were a football team to be reckoned with. They soundly beat the mighty Patriots, 31-13, to move back into a first place tie.

After New England took a 3-0 lead in the first, Joe fired a pair of second period TD passes to Frank Lewis to put his team ahead to stay. The score was 14-13 going into the final session, but the Bills put another 17 points on the board to ice the game. Cribbs atoned for his fumbles the previous week with 118 yards. Joe had a subpar game in the wind with just 12 of 28 for 176 yards.

But the fortunes of war can turn quickly in a long season. At home again the following week against the Atlanta Falcons, the Bills quickly took a 14-0 lead early in the second quarter. But that's all they got. The Falcons stormed back for ten points in each of the final three periods to win, 30-14. Joe outpassed rival quarterback Steve Bartkowski, 270 yards to 193, but yet the club was soundly beaten. After a 5-0 start, the club was now 6-3 and struggling. The next few weeks would probably tell the tale for 1980.

The next one was against the hapless New York Jets, but again the weather was bad and it was raining heavily at Shea Stadium in New York. Joe wasn't having a big day statistically, but he got the team on the board with a pass to Brammer in the first period. He hit his tight end in the end zone again in the second, and it was a 17-10 game at halftime. A Roosevelt Leaks score made it 24-10, but the Jets came back to tie it at 24-all late in the final period.

With 48 seconds left, the Jets got the ball but were forced to punt. Finally, the Bills had it at the Jets 47 with 18 seconds left. Joe then passed 16 yards to Brammer at the 31. With just 12 seconds left he dropped back and fired down the left sideline to Lewis, who made a juggling catch and ran into the end zone for the winning score with just six seconds left. The 31-24 victory hopefully was the tonic the club needed.

A 14-0 shutout of Cincinnati followed, raising the club's record to 8-3 and keeping them a game up on New England. Then in a big one, they soundly defeated the defending Super Bowl champ Steelers, 28-13, scoring once in each period, as the defense played well for the second straight week. Joe had a fine game with 16 of 28 for 212 yards, and outpassed another friend, Terry Bradshaw. Joe hit Jerry Butler with two scoring passes and connected with Reuben Gant for a third.

Then, for a second time, the team came against Baltimore. This one was a 28-24 barnburner and an embarrassing loss because Bert Jones didn't play. The Bills

won the statistical battle, but lost the war. Yet at 9-4
they still had a game edge on New England in the division race.

Now the Bills had to contend with Coach Knox's old
team, the Rams, and this one was close all the way. A
defensive struggle, the game was tied 7-7, at the end of
regulation. Then at 5:14 of the overtime period, Nick
Mike-Meyer booted a 30-yard field goal to win it for the
Bills. Their tenth victory was their best total since 1965
and rookie Cribbs gained 83 yards to go over 1,000 for
the season. Joe was just 10 of 25 for 138 yards against
the tough L.A. defense.

Then came a showdown game with New England, and
trouble. Joe had completed his first two passes when he
went down with an ankle injury, and had to leave the
game. Without him, the Bills were beaten easily, 24-2.
Now they were faced with a must-win situation in the
finale against San Francisco. A loss, and New England
win, goodbye divisional title.

Joe played, the ankle heavily taped. It was obvious he
didn't have real good mobility. Had the division title
already been salted away, he probably would have sat
out and rested for the playoffs. But he got the Bills on
the board first with a 10-yard scoring toss to Butler in
the first period. The kick was missed and the 49ers tied
it up before the end of the period. They, too, missed the
extra point, so it was a 6-6 game.

The Bills took a 13-6 lead at half when Curtis Brown
ran it in from the four. Then in the third period the 49ers
tied it again at 13. A Mike-Meyer field goal gave the
Bills a 16-13 lead, and before the third period ended,
they got a safety, making it 18-13. Then the defense took
over and held the 49ers the rest of the way.

The clutch victory gave the Bills the AFC East title
with an 11-5 mark. Joe was just 12 of 20 for 102 yards in
the finale, but Cribbs had a big day with 128 yards on 18

carries. But the big thing was they won and were in the playoffs.

For the year, Joe hit on 251 of 439 passes for 2,805 yards. He didn't have the yardage of a year earlier, but it was a more balanced and controlled offense. He also had his best completion percentage ever, 57.2, as well as throwing for 20 touchdowns against 18 intercepts. He had done the job.

In the playoffs, the Bills once again had to meet the San Diego Chargers. Joe tried to play down the ankle injury, but it was obvious he wasn't moving well. The injury was aggrevated in the first period as San Diego took a 3-0 lead. Joe had to leave the game briefly for additional taping, but was back in the second period.

He then led the Bills on two scoring drives, Leaks getting the first TD on a one-yard plunge, and Joe passing to Lewis from nine-yards out for the second. The Bills had a 14-3 lead at the half.

But in the latter two periods Joe began losing his effectiveness. He couldn't set up or throw in his usual manner, and the Buffalo defense had to withstand Dan Fouts' blistering air attack. The Chargers got one back in the third to make it 14-10. Then a field goal early in the fourth made it 14-13. Finally, late in the game, Fouts hit substitute wide receiver Ron Smith on a 50-yard touchdown bomb for the winning score. The Chargers won, 20-14.

Joe was 15 of 29 for 180 yards, but he threw three intercepts. He tried not to use the ankle as an excuse, but he told reporters how it affected his game.

"It bothered me," he said. "I couldn't put the usual weight on my left foot. I wasn't able to move around like I thought I could coming into the game. The ankle did shut down our offense a bit, but not a great deal."

There was no way it couldn't have affected Joe and the offense, and it's a shame things had to end like that.

But injuries have always been part of the game. It had still been a great season for both Joe and the Bills, a team that seems to be getting better still. Chuck Knox was voted Coach of the Year, and owner Ralph Wilson proclaimed, "Chuck could give us a dynasty here."

After the long season had finally ended, and the Oakland Raiders wound up the eventual Super Bowl champs, Joe was in Hawaii, taking a bit of a vacation and playing in a golf tournament there. It was mid-February. He said it was the first time he had been able to do anything athletic on the ankle since the final game with San Diego.

"I began running for the first time about a week ago," he said. "I'm still undergoing the same treatment as when I first hurt it—first heat, then ice. But I don't think the ankle will ever be quite the same again. I'll always have to play with it heavily supported."

So it was a severe injury and Joe really gutted it out when he played on it. Though he still hadn't made the Pro Bowl or Super Bowl, he had gained a tremendous amount of respect among his peers, more than even he realized. A large number of NFL players and former players, including Deacon Jones, Randy Rasmussen, and Archie Manning, said the same thing whenever asked. Basically, it was: "Buffalo would have defeated San Diego in the playoffs if Ferguson hadn't hurt his ankle."

And Andy Russell, a former all-pro linebacker with the Steelers, spelled it out even more clearly.

"The Bills would have beaten the Chargers and then I doubt if Oakland could have come out of Buffalo without losing," Russell said. "The Bills could have been in New Orleans (for the Super Bowl) easily if Joe hadn't been injured. It would not have surprised me because I saw them beat the Steelers and they were as impressive a team as I saw all year."

And the team has an impressive quarterback. Joe Ferguson is still underrated and low-key in his approach to the game. But more and more people are appreciating his talents. Joe's life is more settled now than ever before. He married the former Sandi Brown of Shreveport in April of 1980, and has some business interests in his beloved Louisiana. He still relaxes with his horses and his old friends from Woodlawn High.

But come the fall, he'll be back in Buffalo, leading the resurgent Bills toward their long sought after goal. And it will be very appropriate if Joe Ferguson of Natchitoches, Louisiana, can help bring the Super Bowl trophy to the shores of Lake Erie. Both he and the Bills will have earned it.

Steve Bartkowski

When he first came to Atlanta, it looked as if Steve
Bartkowski could become that city's biggest hero since
Rhett Butler. But unlike Butler, the fictional hero of
Margaret Mitchell's *Gone With the Wind*, Steve
Bartkowski's destiny was not determined by the pen of
a novelist. He was a football player, a quarterback, and
as anyone who knows the sport will tell you, a
quarterback's destiny can change with a single sweep of
his throwing arm.

But when Bartkowski arrived, his credentials and
Rhett Butler's were not all that different. While the mysterious Mr. Butler may have had the dark, mysterious,
mustachioed look of his time, Steve Bartkowski had the
look of the 1970's. He was tall, muscular, and had flowing blond curls and a dimpled smile. Butler was a heroic
figure, a military man, engaged in activities surrounding
the Civil War, an event of epic proportions. Bartkowski
was a football hero, a man brought to Atlanta to lead
the fledgling Atlanta Falcons franchise to glory. You
can't get more heroic than that.

Unfortunately, things are rarely as simple as they
seem. Even Rhett Butler would have had his problems if
he had to face mammoth defensive linemen and blitzing
linebackers week in and week out. It's very easy to lose

that dash and charm when you are trying to come back after knee surgery, or being led from the field of battle in a daze after having your bell rung by a blind-side hit. And Rhett Butler never knew what it was like to be booed by some 60,000 fans.

By now, the picture is becoming clear. It has not all been a bed of roses for Steve Bartowski since he came to Atlanta hailed as a saviour in 1975. He has been racked by injury and by inconsistency in his own performance, as well as his team's. Atlanta showed promise on a number of occasions only to disappoint the following year. Steve found himself benched and booed. His personal life suffered. He even contemplated giving up the game if his 6-4, 215-pound body continued to betray him.

But Steve pulled himself together. He rededicated himself. He gave his life to God as a born again Christian and he gave himself to the game of football with renewed vigor. With the Falcons getting some good, young players, Steve Bartkowski again became the focal point, the leader of a balanced, yet explosive offense. He was instrumental in getting the Falcons the 1980 NFC Western Division championship and bringing them into the playoffs.

There are many contrasts in the Steve Bartkowski story. It takes in both the good and the bad of college and professional sports, the rewards as well as the heartaches, and how it can prey on a young athlete's mind. Everybody loves a hero, but people are also quick to jump off the bandwagon when things begin to go sour. And sometimes that can be a great shock to the youngster who has had things his way most of his life.

Steven Joseph Bartkowski was born on November 12, 1952, in Des Moines, Iowa, the only son and eldest child of Roman and Helen Bartkowski, who later had two daughters. Mr. Bartkowski, whom everyone called Bart, was a carpenter by trade, but that wasn't his passion. Besides his family, the thing he loved most was baseball.

He played the game incessantly, and had a dream of playing in the major leagues. A pitcher of note in the Des Moines area, he was signed by the Chicago Cubs organization and went about trying to make it to the bigs. He didn't miss by much, but unfortunately, he never made it past Triple-A ball. That was an accomplishment in itself, the next highest level, but it wasn't good enough for Bart Bartkowski. When Steve was born his father was still toiling in the minors, and would do so until 1954.

The minors were even a harder life then they are today, traveling in buses, staying in below-average hotels and motels, and eating on the run. Plus the pay was barely enough to live on. In the off-season, Mr. Bartkowski did whatever carpentry work he could, but come spring he always wanted to give the diamond one more try.

Of course, when Steve was born it was only natural that the father thought about the future. So when young Steve was barely old enough to walk, Bart had him out on the front lawn swinging at a ball with a light, plastic bat. Steve's athletic training had begun.

"Bart worked very hard teaching baseball to Steve and he did it for a long, long time," Helen Bartkowski recalls. "I used to worry about it from time to time because I didn't want it to become an obsession. But Steve loved it because he got so much attention from his father. None of his friends had fathers who were so interested in them."

Young Steve was small and skinny and he grew very slowly. In fact, when he joined the Little League at about the age of nine, he was still so small that he didn't play very much. But his father was still convinced the boy would grow up to be a great athlete.

By that time, Mr. Bartkowski was no longer playing ball himself, and he began looking for more work as a carpenter. There was usually enough during the summer months, but in the winter things would slow down and the family would have to tighten up on the purse strings. Finally, Mr. and Mrs. Bartkowski made a decision. They would move to a warmer climate and a place where there would be work all year round. So just about the time Steve was finishing elementary school, the family packed up and moved to Santa Clara, California.

"I don't know whether it was a coincidence or what," Mrs. Bartkowski says, "but as soon as we got to California, Steve started growing like a weed and didn't stop."

Once that happened and he began to get some strength and coordination, all his early athletic training began to pay off. He became the best athlete in the neighborhood and at junior high school. In the eighth grade he was already close to his full height of 6-4 and he was filling out fast. Ironically, his father began worrying that he would grow *too* big to play baseball.

By that time, Steve was active in all the sports. He played basketball and football with his friends. His father felt he used the other sports to stay in shape and would soon put the emphasis on baseball once he hit high school.

But it didn't take long after he reached Buscher High in Santa Clara for the school's football coach to notice him. In fact, one look at the big, strapping youngster and the coach asked him to report to practice that same week.

Steve welcomed the idea of playing football for it didn't interfere with baseball season. But his father saw it differently. To him, all football would produce was an injury which would keep him from playing baseball. And because of this he refused to sign the necessary permission form.

"It didn't look as if Dad would change his mind," Steve recalls. "But by then I really wanted to play. A lot of my friends were going out and they wanted me along. So Mom and I became conspirators. She signed her name, then forged his beneath it."

There are two versions of how Mr. Bartkowski discovered Steve was playing football. One has it that Steve came home with an injury to his nose and admitted he got it playing football. Another is that Mrs. Bartkowski told her husband she wanted to go for a ride one day and took him over to see the practice.

At any rate, once Mr. Bartkowski learned that Steve had a good chance at starting quarterback and was able to take care of himself, he finally gave his OK.

Steve was such an outstanding athlete at Buscher High that he became a kind of legend in the area. Some of the stories about him have undoubtedly been exaggerated over the years, for example, it was said that he once heaved the football 103 yards to see how far he could throw it. But some of the legendary stories are true.

It's down on record that he once scored 52 points during a basketball game in which he played only 28 minutes! He also hit a slew of very long home runs. And in his last two years as quarterback on the football team he threw for more than 3,000 yards and had 36 touchdown passes. With a record like that, it's no wonder that scouts and recruiters began hanging around Buscher High and the Bartkowski house.

Mr. Bartkowski had probably dreamed for years about talking to the major league scouts, about his own days in the game, and about his son. But most of the scouts who came were football recruiters, and they tried to talk Steve into coming to their schools. There were some baseball people, and the Kansas City Royals were interested enough to name Steve in their 1971 draft, the same year he was to graduate from Buscher.

Figuring his father would twist his arm to take the Kansas City offer, Steve recalls what happened:

"My father was kind of torn. He obviously wanted me to play baseball and the K.C. offer was very tempting. But he also felt it was important for me to go to college, also. I guess that shows he had changed with the times. In his day, college didn't matter as much, especially if you got a baseball offer. But he finally did the best thing. He told me to decide, to do what *I* wanted, and I've always respected him greatly for that."

But it wasn't easy to decide once the pressuring began. Besides the Kansas City offer, he was deluged with well over 100 football scholarship offers to schools all over the country. Many assumed because he was from Santa Clara, Stanford University would be his first choice. He would follow in the footsteps of another Santa Clara quarterback, Jim Plunkett, who had received a great deal of notoriety as well as the Heisman Trophy for his passing exploits at Stanford.

Steve had to give Stanford a great deal of thought and there was no doubt that they wanted him. Stanford quarterbacks were always well prepared for the NFL since the school's offense closely resembled that of most pro teams. But at the same time Steve was deciding about Stanford, he was also getting pressure from the Kansas City Royals, who began telling him how playing college football could mess up a prospective baseball career.

"They kept reminding me that they had picked me on the first round," Steve recalls, "and that if things went well I could be their regular first baseman within three years."

But if he went to college, Steve preferred to remain in California. He liked the climate and would be close to home. His decision not to attend Stanford was made partly because he would be constantly compared to Jim Plunkett and he didn't want that.

"Plunkett was one of the all-time great quarterbacks," said Steve, "and it wouldn't be easy duplicating what he did. There would be all his records, always staring me in the face. So I looked around some more and began to consider the University of California quite seriously. It dawned on me that Cal was down near the bottom, the same place Stanford was when Plunkett went there. I figured I could be Cal's answer to Jim Plunkett. That's the way I was thinking back then. I'd go to Cal and lead them right into the Rose Bowl."

So in the fall of 1971, Steve Bartkowski packed off to Berkeley and the University of California, where his scholarship would allow him to play both football and baseball. The football team at Cal was rarely above the level of the mediocre. The Golden Bears didn't have the number of top quality players that other Pacific-8 schools, such as USC and UCLA, had. In 1969 they were 5-5, in 1970, 6-5, and in 1971, while Steve was on the freshman team, they were also 6-5.

But while they didn't challenge to so-called top schools, there were always some fine individual players at Cal, especially at the quarterback position. Before Steve, there was Joe Kapp and Craig Morton, both of whom went on to the NFL. And following Steve was the late Joe Roth and the most recent, Rich Campbell.

As a sophomore, Steve split the quarterbacking with another player in the early going, but eventually won the job. The team had a new coach that year, Mike White, and it was rough going. Besides the Pac-8 teams, there was the likes of Colorado, Missouri, and Ohio State. The team wound up 3-8 and Steve learned some hard lessons, being under siege most of the year and taking some bad beatings. His size prevented him from being a terribly mobile quarterback and once his pass protection broke down, he was often a sitting duck.

In 1972, he completed 70 of 165 passes for 944 yards, a passing percentage of just 42.4. He threw four TD passes, and playing catch-up so often, had 13 intercepted. The football season wasn't very enjoyable in a lot of ways but joining the baseball team the following spring, he met with immediate success.

His coach was Jackie Jensen, a former outstanding major league outfielder with the Yankees and Red Sox. Jensen suggested Steve do some catching as well as playing first base and he excelled at both positions. He also flexed his muscles by becoming Cal's greatest single season home run hitter with 12, in addition to hitting well over .300.

His success on the diamond that year far surpassed his gridiron exploits of the past autumn. Major league scouts came from everywhere. They all wanted to sign him.

In the summer, he went to Kansas to play in a semi-pro baseball league. Hitting very well, it began to look as if his father might get his long-time wish after all. Steve seemed to be gravitating toward baseball once again. The situation there seemed so much more positive than in football, because Steve was uncertain whether he'd be the starting QB in 1973.

When White took over, one of his prize recruits was a strong-armed quarterback, Vince Ferragamo, whose style was much like Steve's. And, because White seemed to favor him over Bartkowski, and his successful summer baseball season ending, Steve decided not to report for pre-season football drills. He was on the brink of quitting.

But Coach White didn't want to lose Steve. For one thing a coach is always in need of a backup quarterback because an injury can occur at any time. White wasn't sure that Bartkowski wouldn't win the job. The two had a long talk, and Steve finally agreed to come out for football once again his junior year of 1973.

"I decided to go along with Coach White and commit myself fully to football for the season," was the way Steve put it.

The 1973 Golden Bears had more offensive tools than before. They had an outstanding running back in Chuck Muncie, and a mercurial wide receiver, Wesley Walker.

In constant battle with Ferragamo for the starting position, Steve got the first call. But as soon as he faltered Ferragamo came in and soon got the bulk of the playing time for the rest of the season. The team wasn't much better from the season before. They had improved by one game to 4-7, and were pasted pretty good by their prestigious Pac-8 rivals. UCLA beat them, 61-21, and USC did it by a 50-14 count.

As for Steve, he threw even less than he had as a sophomore, but he actually was more productive. He completed 61 of 129 for 910 yards and a 47.3 percentage. He threw for four more scores and cut his intercepts to seven. But it was far from a satisfying season. He had a different kind of reaction. Instead of thinking about quitting or about baseball, he made a firm resolve to continue with football and win the quarterback job outright for 1974. He even passed up baseball that spring to concentrate on giving football his best shot.

When he returned in the fall he got a surprising bit of news. He wouldn't have to compete for the quarterback job after all. Ferragamo wasn't especially happy at Cal, either, and he decided to transfer to the University of Nebraska. Not that Steve wouldn't have welcomed the competition, but it felt good to know that he would finally get a chance to quarterback the team for the entire season, barring injury, of course.

Steve took charge of the team right away, showed he was the boss, and within a few short weeks the college football world began to ask where he had been hiding for three years. Although the team lost its opener to Florida, 21-17, they whipped San Jose State and Army, toppled Illinois, 31-14, and Oregon, 40-10.

After whipping Oregon State they were toppled by a powerful UCLA team, 28-3, but bounced right back to tie an equally tough USC club, 15-15. The pro scouts couldn't take their eyes off the big guy from Santa Clara.

"Bartkowski has strength, poise, leadership ability, and a rocket for an arm," said one scout. "Looks to me like he's ready to step into the pros without too much of a transition. He's playing like a pro already."

"Best collegiate quarterback I've seen all year," said another. "He stands tall in the pocket, doesn't rattle, and hits receivers short and long. Definitely NFL caliber."

When the team defeated Washington, 52-26, Steve made headlines by throwing for 316 yards. A week later, in a 37-33 win over Washington State, *Sports Illustrated* Magazine named him College Football Offensive Player of the Week. And finally, in his last game, he racked up another 318 passing yards, as the team lost a 22-20 squeaker to Stanford.

In the space of a single year, Steve had gone from a second-stringer to the nation's leading passer. He was a consensus All-American at his position, *the* college quarterback of 1974. His statistics were awesome.

First, he led the Bears to a 7-3-1 record, their best in years. He did it by completing 182 of 325 passes for 2,580 yards. His completion percentage was way up to 56.0, and he threw for 12 touchdowns, while tossing just seven interceptions. Quite impressive numbers. He had four, 300-yard games, and set several California and Pac-8 records. Thoughts of a baseball career were now all but gone. For Steve, the National Football League was the next step.

It took awhile for his great season to really sink in, for both Steve and others. For one thing, California had been on probation by the NCAA during Steve's three varsity seasons, meaning the team couldn't appear on national television, nor were they eligible for bowl games. But his yardage total was best in the nation among the major colleges and his seven interceptions in 325 attempts was an incredibly low number. So Steve really made an impression. One who discovered Steve early was Norm Pellom of the nearby Los Angeles Rams. He first spotted the big guy when he was splitting time as a junior.

"I don't care who makes All-America," Pellom said, during Steve's senior year. "Right now Steve Bartkowski gets top marks for delivery, size, timing, poise, and vision. He's the top college quarterback in the country. A year ago he was a good prospect. This year he's a brilliant prospect."

Other reports were just as glowing, especially as the season wore on, and Steve was on the minds of a number of National Football League teams. This was all extremely exciting for Steve. He had never received this kind of attention or acclaim, and he anxiously awaited the annual college draft for 1975. He was hoping he'd be picked on the first round.

The team that had the first choice in the draft was the Baltimore Colts. But the Colts didn't need a quarterback, they were run by the brilliant Bert Jones. But like all teams with the top choice, they dangled the choice in the air to see if any other clubs would come up with a suitable deal.

The Atlanta Falcons offered their all-pro offensive tackle, George Kunz. Because the Colts needed a tackle to solidify their offensive line and protect Jones, they jumped at the chance to pick up one of the very best.

The Falcons now had the number one choice. And on

the day of the draft they exercised it by choosing Steve
Bartkowski. It was just incredible for him. First his suc-
cess at Cal, now the prestigious first choice of the entire
National football League. He was overjoyed.

"I always wanted to play either in California or the
South," he said. "They take their football very seriously
in California, and I hear they take it even more seriously
in the South. I'm really pleased to be their selection.

"You know, it's hard to believe all this is happening
to me. It's such a new experience, but I'm going to enjoy
it, the whole thing."

Later, when he got his bearings and had settled down
a bit, he was able to joke with reporters about his selection.

"How many of you know that of the last four guys
taken first in the draft, three of them were Polish?" he
quipped. "There was Walt Patulski, John Matuszak,
and now Steve Bartkowski. The only guy who broke the
streak was Too Tall Jones. When I meet him I'm gonna
ask if I can call him Too Tall Joneski."

So it was a gala time for Steve. Before long he was
headed to Atlanta to meet the coaching staff and talk
about his first professional contract.

Because of his excitement and boyish exuberance,
Steve might not have given too much thought to the situation he was heading for. The Falcons were not a good
football team. They were an expansion team, formed
back in 1966, and like most expansion teams, the early
years were not easy. The first three seasons the team was
in the league it posted records of 3-11, 1-12-1, and 2-12.

There was a glimmer of hope when Norm Van
Brocklin, a former quarterback great, took over as
coach during the 1968 season. The club seemed to be
improving and posted its first winning season in 1971,
with a 7-6-1 log. Two years later Van Brocklin surprised
the football world by bringing the Falcons home at 9-5,

and a second-place finish in the NFC Western Division.

But just when it seemed as if the franchise had achieved respectability, the team plummeted again. They nosedived all the way back to 3-11 in 1974, as Van Brocklin was fired and defensive coordinator Marion Campbell got the job. The 9-5 finish must have been something of a fluke. The team just wasn't that good. There weren't enough quality players and little precious depth. So Steve would be joining a club that was going into its tenth season in the league and was still not a consistent winner.

There are two ways for a young quarterback to look at this particular kind of situation. Joining a weak team, he's got more of a chance to play right away. He can learn on the job and grow with the team, but he's going to take his lumps along the way, both mental and physical. If he can survive them, he's got a chance to make it. Joining an established winner, there's more of a chance the young signal-caller will be brought along slowly, eased into the lineup behind an experienced veteran. Most youngsters want to play, but in a tough situation they can really have rough going.

But at this point, Steve Bartkowski was living the American Dream. There was a bit of a hassle over his signing, but it was finally resolved and when he signed, he had become the highest-paid rookie to that time in NFL history, getting some $650,000 over four years. (Joe Namath's fabled first contract with the New York Jets was in the old AFL.)

Steve's arrival in Atlanta was treated like the Second Coming. He was proclaimed the team's saviour, an instant hero before he had thrown a single pass in anger. He was even given a nickname equated with Namath's "Broadway Joe." They dubbed Steve, "Peachtree Bart," in reference to Peachtree Street, where it all happened in Atlanta. Whether he knew it or not, the Falcon fans were already expecting miracles, and in effect putting a great deal of pressure on his shoulders.

Before reporting to his first pro training camp, Steve went to Chicago to play in the annual College All-Star Game. That was the game in which the best of the rookie collegians played against the previous year's Super Bowl Winner. The "annual" game is no longer played because the collegians rarely won and no one really benefited by it.

In 1975, Steve found himself going up against the Steel Curtain defense of the Pittsburgh Steelers, featuring the likes of Mean Joe Greene, L.C. Greenwood, Jack Lambert, Mel Blount, and the rest of that magnificent cast. It was enough to send any collegian packing.

Fortunately, the Steelers weren't very sharp offensively, and while the defense wasn't in mid-season form, they were tough enough. It was a low-scoring game. As the evening unfolded, the only player providing the All-Stars with any offense was Steve Bartkowski. Several times he had the Stars moving under his direction and his fine passing.

In the first period he calmly tossed a 28-yard touchdown pass to Pat McInally, and by the fourth period he actually had the All-Stars ahead, 14-7. The Steelers sucked it in and drove for a pair of late scores to win the game, 21-14, but Steve was the All-Stars MVP.

He had completed seven of 18 passes for 126 yards against the Steel Curtain. And what made it even more impressive was the fact that the Stars had virtually no running attack, amassing a grand total of 19 yards on the ground for the night. And 16 of those came from a rookie back named Walter Payton, who was destined to get a few more in the ensuing years.

When Steve finally hit the Falcons' camp, he was more of the hero than ever. And he began to live up to it immediately. It wasn't long before he had obviously won the starting job, and he was looking good. Though Steve didn't know it at the time, he was about to embark of the most emotionally filled year of his life to that time.

Coming to the Falcons also in 1975 were two small, but talented wide receivers, Alfred Jenkins and Wallace Francis. There was also a good, veteran tight end in Jim Mitchell. The running attack was just adequate, with veteran Dave Hampton, nearing the end of the line, and Haskel Stanback the best performers. Kim McQuilken of Lehigh was the backup quarterback.

Yet from the beginning of the season, Steve seemed to work magic on the offense. He had them moving, was providing leadership and confidence, and he was executing very well. His strong arm was undoubtedly of major league caliber, he seemed to read defenses well for a rookie quarterback, and had the knack of coming up with the big play when it was needed.

The team came close in its first two games, losing to St. Louis, 23-20, and Detroit, 17-14. Then Steve got them on the board, as the Falcons toppled New Orleans, 14-7, and San Francisco, 17-3. The only problem was that late in the 49er game, he was hit hard by a couple of defensive linemen and was led off the field with an injured elbow.

His injury would cause him to miss four weeks. During his absence, the team lost to Los Angeles, Cincinnati, New Orleans and Minnesota by a combined score of 104-28. They were just not the same team without Steve Bartkowski at the helm.

In just a few short weeks Steve had earned the total respect of his teammates, running the offense like a seasoned veteran. He was also getting a great deal of attention from the media wherever the team went, yet there didn't seem to be any noticeable jealousy of that or the size of his contract. He seemed to have fit in very well for a raw rookie.

Fortunately, the injury was to the left elbow, not his throwing arm, but he still had to wear a light cast for a couple of weeks. He continued to travel with the team and before a game in New Orleans, Coach Campbell found Steve trying to suit up despite the injured arm. Their conversation went this way:

"What do you think you're doing?" the coach asked.

"Dressing," said Bartkowski, without skipping a beat.

"What for?" asked the surprised coach.

"Because there might be some way I can help out there."

The coach laughed. "Forget it," he said. "Even if we let you dress the officials would run you off the field because of the cast on your elbow."

But that was Steve's attitude as a rookie. He would do anything to help the team. The coach knew how valuable his young quarterback was. When the club had dropped their third straight after Steve was injured, a reporter asked what the Falcons needed to get back to their winning ways.

"Number ten," the Coach said, quickly, referring to Steve's uniform number.

What he really wanted was the man in the uniform. He got him back in a rematch with the Rams, but Atlanta lost again, 16-7. The next week, however, Steve had a big day, passing for a pair of touchdowns as the team finally came up big, beating Denver, 35-21. They lost a close one to Oakland in overtime, 37-34. A week later, they were nosed out by Washington, 30-27. Both clubs were powerful and were expected to beat the Falcons handily.

Steve directed the club to a big, 31-9 victory over the

49ers. A week later, the season ended as Green Bay whipped the Falcons, 22-13. The club finished at 4-10, which was on the surface seemed like another dismal season, but this time there was a big reason to be hopeful.

That reason was Steve Bartkowski. He seemed to offer just the tonic the offense needed. In the team games Steve played the Falcons were 4-6 and actually outscored the opposition for those ten games. The four games he missed saw the team buried in each.

Statistically, he had a fine season, completing 115 of 255 passes for 1,662 yards. His passing percentage wasn't good at 45.1, but he had thrown for 13 touchdowns. And considering the team was often behind, his 15 intercepts were not all that bad. Steve was voted the Bert Bell Memorial Trophy as Offensive Rookie of the Year, and also won the *Sporting News* Rookie of the Year award. His future seemed unlimited.

Unfortunately, the unbelievable whirl Steve had been in since arriving in Atlanta resulted in some other things that might have been more difficult to handle than three or four blitzing defenders. On the team flight to San Francisco for the game in which Steve hurt his elbow, he had met a very pretty stewardess. "It was love at first sight," Steve was to say.

After a whirlwind courtship the couple was married during the season and it was one of Atlanta's big social events. It seemed that everything was happening to Steve at once. When the season ended and he was presented with awards, it seemed as if he was a young man who had everything. But all did not fair well as things began to sour.

For one thing, his marriage was in trouble. Steve and his wife soon realized that they really didn't know each other. There was a tremendous demand on Steve's time. Everybody wanted him as Atlanta's newest hero. *I BE-*

LIEVE IN STEVE bumper stickers began appearing on cars all over the city. His agent, Leigh Steinberg, had him moving from one appearance to another. He was asked to be honorary chairman for numerous charities. The whole thing was rapidly becoming unnerving and exhausting, and caused a tremendous strain on his marriage.

Then, after just a few short months, his marriage ended in a quick divorce.

"We both realized it was a foolish mistake," Steve admitted. "We didn't know each other long enough and didn't realize the pressure and responsibility we'd have. We know now that divorce was the best thing for both of us."

Emotionally and physically drained, he began living the life of a bachelor once again. Before his marriage he was already the most eligible young bachelor in the city. Now he was free again. But he wasn't ready to handle it all.

Shortly after his divorce he was stopped in the wee hours of the morning for driving under the influence. It was an embarassing incident.

"I learned my lesson," he said later. "You won't ever catch me driving at that hour again. But in a big singles city like Atlanta, there are a lot of places to go. It's the kind of thing that could happen to anyone, but I'm going to be more careful from now on."

He also had to curtail his schedule. "It got to the point where I'd have two appearances scheduled at the same time one day. I guess I had a hard time saying no to people. One day Tommy Nobis (the Falcons' all-pro linebacker) sat down and had a talk with me. He convinced me to slow down and channel my time into one charity, not all of them. So I finally told my agent, enough, this has got to stop; it's killing me. So now I put all my time into the United Way, and that's it."

Steve was also beginning to realize that being the big hero wasn't everything it's often cracked up to be. But he was man enough to admit:

"It was all so easy for me at the beginning. I was gullible and naive. I read where I was the next Joe Namath and I believed it. And I know a lot of people think it is easy. They say, 'Hey, he's got it made. He's the big quarterback and he can go out every night and get any girl he wants.' That's just stupid. There aren't that many people who will accept me for what I am. It's nice to find someone who's intellectually inclined rather than the kind who just sit and keep saying something silly like, 'Gee, you really are a good football player.' "

So by the time the football season drew near again, Steve Bartkowski had really been through the mill. But he tried to look at the bright side.

"If there's anything positive to all of it," he said, "it's that it all happened during the off-season. I feel as if I've lived 12 years in about four months. Had it happened during the season it would have been extremely difficult to concentrate 100 percent on football. There was too much going on. But I feel it's all behind me now and I'm treating it as an experience, not a problem. And I feel as if I learned a lot from it."

And finally, Steve Bartkowski was able to begin talking like a quarterback and an athlete again.

"Now I'm just looking forward to the season. There are too many people depending on me to do the job and I don't want to let them down. I'm ready to win some football games, get us in the playoffs, and go to the Super Bowl. Unless I have a bad day, I don't see how we can miss."

It was good to hear the old confidence again. But the problem to overcome was that the Falcons still had a good number of weaknesses as a team. They lost their first two games to Los Angeles and Detroit. A victory

over Chicago followed, then a loss to Phildelphia. Steve
wasn't going badly, but he wasn't really playing any better than he had the year before and the team didn't seem
to be rallying behind him in quite the same way.

Then came the fifth game at New Orleans. The Saints
were an expansion team like the Falcons and there was
an intense rivalry between the two. This time, New Orleans was really putting it to Atlanta. Steve tried to rally
the club, but couldn't. Midway through the game he
went down and didn't get up. He was removed from the
game after the trainer and doctor looked at him, and a
subsequent examination revealed cartilege damage to
the right knee. Surgery was necessary and Steve would
be out for the year.

It was a bitter blow. The team had lost the game, 30-0,
and their quarterback as well. And later that same week
their coach was dismissed and General Manager Pat
Peppler took over as interim coach to finish the season,
which was to be another 4-10 campaign.

As for Steve, he played in just five games, completing
57 of 120 passes for 677 yards and a 47.5 percentage. He
had just two touchdowns passes and threw nine interceptions. From his rapid rise to glory from his senior
year in college to the operating table, everything was
suddenly turning in an equally rapid nose dive.

Before the 1977 season, the Falcons made more
changes at the management level, hoping to stabilize the
franchise. Leeman Bennett was the new coach and
former NFL quarterback Eddie LeBaron the general
manager. In the draft, the club looked for help in the
line and on defense. They felt confident in selecting
tackle Warren Bryant, defensive tackle Wilson Fou-
muina, defensive end and tackle Edgar field, and linebacker Robert Pennywell. They also signed a free agent
quarterback by the name of June Jones, III. And veteran
QB Scott Hunter, who had finished the last season when

Steve was hurt, was also back in camp.

Steve's biggest concern was getting the knee ready for the opener. Things seemed to be going well, but then in the middle of the preseason he hurt the knee again. It wasn't as serious as the first time, when there was some ligament damage as well as the cartilege. But there was another cartilege tear on the other side and he needed surgery once again. This one was relatively minor and the hope was he could return sometime during the second half of the season.

Bitter blow number two, especially coming just when he thought he was beginning to come back from the first injury. Now he had to do it all over again. And while he was out, the Falcons began looking like an improved team. With Scott Hunter at the controls, they upset the powerful Rams in the opener, 17-6, lost the Redskins, but then beat the New York Giants and the 49ers. The club was at 3-1, playing winning football, though much of the credit for the improvement had to go to the defense, which was finally keeping the opponents scores very respectable.

In fact, game five was a 3-0 loss to Buffalo, and in those five games the Falcon defense yielded just 22 points. That was about the best mark in the league to that point. The team then split its next two games, beating Chicago and losing to Minnesota. At the halfway point the club was at 4-3, and surprised everyone.

The next week, Steve was reactivated and would be starting. Asked why he was switching back to Bartkowski when the team had done so unexpectedly well under Hunter, Coach Bennett said:

"We feel we can win with our other quarterbacks," the coach said, "but to win big, Steve is the man and he has to play up to his potential."

It didn't happen during the second half of '77, and Steve didn't play exceptionally well. The defense continued to carry the team as they wound up with an improved, 7-7, record. The defense had yielded just 129 points in 14 games, best mark in the league, and down from the 312 of a year earlier.

As for Steve, he completed just 64 of 136 passes for 796 yards, a 47.1 passing percentage, five touchdowns and 13 interceptions. One interesting statistic showed that the Atlanta quarterbacks were sacked just 11 times in the first seven games, but Steve was sacked 29 times in the final seven. Word was that he lacked mobility and because of his injuries was a bit reluctant to fight off the pass rush the way he used to be.

"I probably came back sooner than I should have," he admitted. "My knee wasn't as strong as it should have been and I was aware of it."

But for the first time there were also some doubts about Steve's ultimate ability. Though he had been hurt in each of his first three seasons, he had yet to complete 50 percent of his passes, and that was not a good sign. Though he obviously had the big arm, perhaps he lacked some of the so-called intangibles, like the ability to pick up secondary receivers, and the natural instincts to know where his receivers would be on a broken play. Steve himself was very depressed about the entire situation and felt some of the blame might have to go to the Atlanta organization itself.

"The whole thing about me going number one in the draft is really a farce," he said. "I know that now. And it's not so much that you need to be drafted by a contender, but rather by an organization that's sound, one that is building. With three different coaches and a whole change in the front office, that doesn't make it easy for a young kid to adjust. And it hasn't been a situation that's conducive to playing good football."

But he also admitted he hadn't played his best ball since coming to the Falcons.

"No, I haven't played to my capability since I've been here," he said. "And that includes my rookie year. Now, my goal is just to get in a full season. I don't want to be one of these guys who hangs around for 10 or 12 years and never finds out how good he can be. In that respect, it's really been a frustrating three seasons."

So Steve went back to California and worked, spending a great deal of time at a Rehabilitation Clinic near his home.

"I worked at strengthening my right knee three days a week for four months," he explained. "At one point I thought I had messed it up again. The knee really swelled up and I didn't think it was responding. But the people at the rehab center said that was normal and it would go down. They were right, but it was an anxious three weeks before it felt right again. Then it began gaining strength."

Once the knee was strong enough, Steve began playing racquetball and running some seven to ten miles a day. The racquetball was for his quickness, which he hoped would improve his ability to handle the pass rush and move around a bit better. This seemed to be a major concern with the Atlanta people, and they were voicing some doubt for the first time whether Steve was the quarterback who would bring the club respectability and hopefully an eventual crack at the Super Bowl.

When General Manager Eddie LeBaron talked about the team in '78, he mentioned that the Falcons felt they were building one of the best young offensive lines in the league. Then he added, "And that young line should help our quarterbacks."

When questioned why he had said "quarterbacks" when it was assumed that Steve was still number one, LeBaron answered:

"Steve has lost some mobility because of his knee surgery. He never was the fastest man around. He obviously has a Super Bowl arm, but in this league a quarterback must be able to move, as well. We know he's been working very hard in the off season and wants desperately to prove himself. Let's just say we're all hoping for him."

But when Steve arrived in camp that July, he was optimistic, yet because of recent history, he tempered it a bit.

"I feel great," he said, "but then, I've felt the same way every other summer. Each year, I've come to camp ready to go. When I came off the program at the rehab center my right knee tested 102 percent compared to my left. So I hope that's all behind me. I'm determined not to let the pass rush bother me. Standing in there against it has always been one of my strengths. I really worked hard in the off season and I'm determined to come back with a sound knee and play well."

The team continued to build. Several new players made the club, notably wide receiver Alfred Jackson and defensive back Tom Pridemore, as well as a free agent placekicker named Tim Mazzetti. And in camp the coaches were really excited about the way Steve Bartkowski was running the offense and throwing the football.

Then came the first preseason game against the New York Jets. Steve started and looked awful. He was unsure and tentative, and he had completed just five of 11 passes for a mere 25 yards when he came out. The Falcons trailed by a 17-0 count, until back-up June Jones came in and hit on six of 11 for 144 yards and two scores, as the team rallied to win it, 20-17.

The next week Steve didn't play. Scott Hunter and Kim McQuilken got the call against Pittsburgh. Next came a game with the Eagles at Atlanta, where the public had suddenly turned sour on Steve as well.

"It's hard to understand," Coach Bennett said, "but

the fans seem to have gotten down on Steve. I guess they expected him to be our saviour and that's asking an awful lot of anyone. After all, he's just part of our team. He can't be expected to do it alone."

But the coach also made it clear that Steve's start against the Eagles would be a very crucial test for him, perhaps putting him under the most pressure since he arrived in Atlanta.

"I've got to find out about him," said Bennett. "He's been hurt so often in his three seasons that he's really little more than a rookie. I've told Steve this is an important game. I'm not saying it's over for him if he doesn't do well, but this is the time for him to come in and execute like a quarterback is supposed to execute. Plus Steve has to find out about himself and he'll only do it by playing."

The game turned into a complete disaster for both Steve and the Falcons. Bennett let his quarterback go all the way. It didn't help Steve any, either, that the fans booed him unmercifully throughout the game. It was the first time in his entire football career that he had received that kind of treatment from a home crowd.

The first half was fairly respectable, though the Falcons began missing opportunities. Steve was six of 14 for 99 yards in the first two periods, and he had enough time to throw. He threw one very bad pass at the end of the second period when the Falcons got in close. Instead of looking for a secondary receiver or a back, he threw for tight end Jim Mitchell in the end zone. Mitchell was surrounded by Eagles and the ball was intercepted. But the score was still close, the Falcons trailing, 10-7.

In the second half it went from bad to worse. On their first four possessions, the Falcons got the ball on their own 20, 13, 11 and 16 yard lines. Three times, once in each of the first three possessions, Steve was sacked to stop any hint of a drive. The fourth time he threw the

ball poorly and it was picked off and run back for a
Philly score to make it 17-7.

In the fourth period the Eagles just teed off on Steve.
He was sacked again and again. He did connect with
Alfred Jackson on a 53-yarder, but it was brought back
by a tripping penalty. The game ended with the score
24-7 and the fans shouted derisive remarks to Steve as he
left the field. As one Atlanta writer put it:

"The beloved Golden Boy of three years ago is now
the man they love to hate."

And when it was over, Steve Bartkowski sat in the
locker room and cried, as he opened himself up to reporters.

"I've stayed by myself since I returned to Atlanta," he
said. "I don't go out because I don't want any hassles. I
try not to look into people's faces when I do go out
because I don't want them to recognize me. I can't be
myself and I find myself living in a shell."

When his mother read a story about the Eagles game
being Steve's last chance, she immediately called him.

"That really got to me," Steve said. "I was thinking
what did I do to deserve a one-game ultimatum. I didn't
sleep two nights before the game. I was tied up in knots.
To tell the truth, I'm really fed up with everything. Last
week was a real burden and I'm glad it's over, no matter
what.

"I don't really mind the booing except for the way it
affects my teammates. Plus the fans don't really know
what's going on out on the field. But the young guys
could be thinking, 'hey, if the fans are booing, maybe
this guy is really bad.' And I'm sure some of my teammates and the coaches have lost some faith in me. That's
upsetting. But I don't play football for those people in
the stands. And if I'm tentative, it's because I've been in
the hospital three years running."

It was a real crisis. Steve even acknowledged that

perhaps he had worn out his welcome in Atlanta, adding that the team would let him know when his services were no longer needed. Then in the final preseason game against Washington, Jones played all the way and led the Falcons to a 10-7 victory. The handwriting was on the wall. Two days later Coach Bennett announced that June Jones would be the Falcons' starting quarterback in the opening game against Houston. Steve Bartkowski had lost his job.

He tried to be philosophical, yet still confident. "I'm relieved because this takes the pressure off me," he said. "But I just don't know how much justice there is. You get all of the credit or all of the blame. But I don't think there's any doubt that I'm the better quarterback."

The club opened the 1978 season against Houston with June Jones at quarterback and promptly won a 20-14 decision over a very good Oilers team. Reports said that Steve sat on his helmet away from the Atlanta bench and "pouted." But during this time there was a very big change taking place within him.

"When everything's going well, you just ride the crest and don't worry about anything," he said, a bit later. "The Lord tried to get through to me by saying you better get off your butt."

Steve had been reading the Bible again for the first time in years. He had been raised in a staunch Catholic family, but now he was finding himself "recommitted."

The next week Jones went all the way again, but the Falcons lost to the Rams, 10-0. The quarterback did not play well, but Jones was now having another kind of influence upon Steve.

"Christ helped me through three colleges," Jones said. "It's exciting to see the difference He's made in Steve. He tried it the other way for three years and all it got him was benched. Steve's a better quarterback than I am. I've known that all along. But the L.A. game I told

Steve, 'Give yourself to God,' and he has."

It was true. Steve had become what is now called a Born Again Christian, rededicating his life to God. He said it was helping him become a better, more peaceful person within himself.

"I've changed my whole life around," Steve said. "I had made the mistake of putting myself first. Now I'm putting the Lord first. When you've exhausted everywhere else to turn, you look someplace to give you strength. Before, I was always saying how could this happen to me? But if I were being a Christian, I'd say this was happening for a reason."

Perhaps it was Steve's turn to religion that gave him the strength to ride out the storm. He could have quit, mentally or physically, or both.

"It wasn't in my upbringing to quit," he said. "My Dad taught me that, and I've always had a lot of pride in being able to bounce back from adversity."

Although Jones completed just five of 15 passes for 38 yards against the Rams, Coach Bennett gave him another shot the following week against Cleveland. Once again the Falcons fell behind early and Jones wasn't capable of bringing them back. Finally, midway through the second half, Bennett turned to Bartkowski for the first time all year, and Steve played well. He threw the ball with authority and seemed to be in control of the offense. Even though the Falcons lost, 24-16, Steve had made an impression. After the game, Coach Bennett said Steve would be starting the following week against Tampa Bay.

"We need something to hype our offense," the coach said. "Steve has a chance to do that. His arm's more live and he played much better than June in the Browns game. But to keep the job, Steve has to play up to his ability. He looked like he was doing that against Cleveland."

As for Steve, he was very happy to get another chance and this time he felt he would do something with it.

"I just have a feeling we're going to click this time. I don't feel the same kind of pressure I felt before. Maybe it's because I know what it's like not to succeed. I've experienced the worst and I think I can handle things from now on."

Against the tough Tampa Bay defense Steve played pretty well. He didn't set the world on fire, but considering his recent idle time, it had to be looked upon as a good sign. The Falcons lost it, 14-9, as Steve went 12 for 24 with a touchdown. But he only threw for 82 yards and was picked off three times. Yet he showed poise and leadership and Coach Bennett decided to stick with him.

"Steve has more ability than our other quarterbacks," the coach said, "but he's got to learn not to try to over-excel. He's got to play to his ability and use the ten other guys, not try to win it himself. That's a problem many young quarterbacks seem to have."

The following week against the New York Giants, Steve led the Falcons to a 23-20 victory. The following week they lost to the mighty Steelers, 31-7, but bounced back to whip Detroit, 14-0. Steve seemed to be gaining in confidence with each passing week. Then came the 49ers out on the Coast, and it was during this game that Steve Bartkowski came of age.

It was a tough defensive battle most of the way. With just eight minutes remaining in the final period, the 49ers forged into a 17-7 lead. It was now or never, and this time Steve faced the situation squarely and took the bull by the horns. First, he dropped back, stepped into the pocket, and rifled a long pass right on the money to Alfred Jackson for a 71-yard gain. The completion set up a Falcons field goal that made the score 17-10.

The next time Atlanta got the ball he moved them quickly to the San Francisco 41. From there, Steve dropped back and looked deep again. Spotting Billy Ryckman streaking down the sideline, he let go arching the ball high and deep . . . and right on target. Ryckman gathered it in on the run and rambled into the end zone. The extra point tied the game at 17-17, with just minutes left.

When the Falcon defenses held, Steve had still another chance. He moved the club by mixing runs and short passes. Then came the key play, a clutch, third-down pass to tight end Mitchell, good for 22 yards. The pass brought the ball in close enough for Tim Mazzetti to boot the winning field goal. The Falcons had come back to take it by a 20-17 score.

And the man of the hour was Steve Bartkowski. The big guy had perhaps his greatest game as a pro, hitting on 15 of 20 passes for 256 yards. Since getting his starting job back, Steve was 57 of 96 for 832 yards and five touchdowns. His performance prompted this comment from Leeman Bennett.

"Steve Bartkowski right now is playing as well as any quarterback in the NFL."

Bennett was not just whistling Dixie about his own man. Steve suddenly had the confidence that he could go out and beat anyone. And he went out and proved it the next week, leading the Falcons past the tough Rams, 15-7. During that game, Steve suffered a separated left shoulder after a seven-yard scramble. At first, they thought he'd be on the shelf. But he was back the following week, leading his club past the 49ers once more, 21-10.

It was the club's fourth straight victory and brought their record to 6-4 after a 1-3 start. Suddenly the Falcons were thinking playoffs. They beat New Orleans the next week, before being derailed by Chicago, 13-7. The team split its remaining four games, beating the Saints again, and Washington, but losing to both Cincinnati and St.

Louis, mainly due to defensive breakdowns. Still, the Falcons had surprised everyone, finishing at 9-7, good for second in the NFC West, and better than that, they had made the playoffs as a wildcard team!

The key to the Falcons' season had been the outstanding year for Steve Bartkowski. The potential had finally become a reality. The stats were much improved. He completed 187 of 369 passes for 2,489 yards, a 50.7 completion percentage, 10 touchdowns and 18 intercepts. He was also a clutch performer. Four times he threw game-tying passes on the team's final possession.

There is no time to rest between the last game of the season and the wildcard game. The following week, Atlanta was on the field again to meet the Philadelphia Eagles, another up-and-coming team and a rugged defensive club. In the first half, the Philadelphia defense dominated the game. Steve couldn't move the Falcons and the Eagles cruised to a 13-0 lead. The big quarterback had hit on only five of 12 passes for 50 yards in the first two sessions.

In the past, such a performance might have prompted a change in quarterbacks. But not anymore. Coach Bennett never even thought about making a change. He had complete confidence in Steve as did the rest of the club. If they kept playing their game they would eventually penetrate the Eagles defense. The only problem was doing it before the clock ran out.

The Falcons waited until late in the game to strike, although Steve had been warming up during the third and fourth sessions and was hitting his receivers and moving the team. He had the club driving again midway through the final period. Then with just under five minutes left the ball was on the Philly 19.

Steve darted back, looked quickly downfield, and fired a touchdown strike to Jim Mitchell. Mazzetti's kick made it a 13-7 game. The Eagles then tried to get a drive going, but the Falcon defense held, and after a punt, Steve and his offense had the ball again for what might be their final shot.

Once again he moved the club with poise and confidence. It was hard to believe this was the same quarterback who had lost his job in the preseason because of ineffectiveness. Now the team responded to his crisp commands, the offensive line firing out hard and pushing the Eagle defenders back toward their own goal line.

With just 1:39 left in the game, the ball was on the Philadelphia 37-yard line. Steve felt he had to go for it. He took the snap, retreated into the pocket, and looked downfield. He spotted wide receiver Wallace Francis over the middle and fired. Bulls-Eye! Francis gathered the ball in as he crossed the goal line for the tying score. Mazzetti's kick gave the Falcons the lead, 14-13. Philly tried for a last-second field goal, but missed. Atlanta had won its first playoff game ever, and its hero was Mr. Steve Bartkowski.

In the second half alone, he had thrown for 193 yards on 13 of 20, and finished the day with 18 of 32 for 243 yards, a clutch performance in the biggest game of his life to date. Now the Falcons would move into the NFC semi-finals against the always powerful Dallas Cowboys. But Steve and his teammates were confident.

"I think the thing that typifies our team is its togetherness," said Steve. "We've got a bunch of guys here who really care about each other, believe in each other, and we also believe we can beat the Dallas Cowboys. It's just this kind of attitude that has brought us as far as we have come this year."

Well, they almost did it. They played the high-favored Cowboys tough all the way, actually leading them, 20-13, at the half. But like all very great teams, the Cowboys have the ability to dig a little deeper when they must, and they pulled out a 27-20 victory. The Falcons season was over. But the team and its quarterback had come a lot further than anyone would have imagined, and now they seemed to be one of the fine, upcoming teams in the NFL.

The team continued to build. One weakness in '78 was the running game, and the '79 draft brought two potentially fine runners, William Andrews of Auburn and Lynn Cain of USC. Steve would remain at quarterback. That was cemented in July, when Steve signed a new, four-year pact, estimated to be worth about $1 million, making him one of the highest paid signal-callers in the game. He really looked forward to the new year.

"My first three years I got away with a lot of things because God gave me a strong arm," he said. "But up until last year I hadn't really done anything in the NFL. I made Rookie of the Year just on raw ability. I didn't know what I was doing. The thing I needed more than anything else was to have a healthy season.

"When I went home in prior years, people didn't even know Atlanta had a football team. Last year it was a bit different. We established a name for ourselves. We've gone from a low-league team that other teams couldn't wait to play on Sunday, to a team that other people are really frightened of."

The 1979 season turned into a very strange one for the Falcons, and, in effect, for Steve. It was the first time they were expected to win, and perhaps that put more pressure on the team. Or perhaps they were a team still a step or two away from really finding themselves. They won their first game against New Orleans, 40-34, and unveiled a new star, rookie runner William Andrews, who surprised even his teammates by running for 167 yards on 30 carries. With veteran Bubba Bean getting 75 more, the Falcons suddenly had a running game.

But even with the running, Steve looked great by hitting on 22 of 38 passes for 312 big yards and a score. It was his greatest day as a pro as the Falcons put 512 yards total offense on the board. The game was decided in overtime on a pass interception and TD run by defensive back James Mayberry.

When the team beat Philly a week later with Andrews running for 121 yards and Steve passing for the winning score to Wallace Francis, it looked as if the Falcons finally had the offensive balance they had been looking for. To everyone surrounding the team, a big year was in the offing.

In the next game, Steve was absolutely brilliant. He set another team mark by completing 20 of 29 passes for 326 yards and two scores. But the Denver Broncos shut down Andrews and the running game, and managed a 20-17 victory in overtime. Still, it seemed as if there was no reason to panic. But the next week came another close loss, 24-23, to Detroit. Steve had a quiet day with 12 of 25 for 158 yards. The Falcons felt they should have had this one. It was the first indication that perhaps this was not going to be the glorious season everyone envisioned.

Game five was a disaster. Steve played terribly against the Washington Redskins. They sacked him three times and his passes were off the mark all day. After two, 300-yard games the first three weeks, he hit on just six of 26 for 105 yards in this one as the club lost, 16-7. It was hard to figure what was happening.

They untracked it the next week, 25-7, over Green Bay, but were then buried by Oakland, 50-19, despite a 20 for 35, 260-yard day by Steve. It was the team's worse loss since 1976, and when they were upset by the 49ers, 20-15, the following week, the club saw half the season gone and had a very disappointing, 3-5, record. Steve had another sub-par day against the 49ers, hitting on just 13 of 27 for 126 yards. He seemed to have returned to the inconsistency of earlier years.

That was the theme of the rest of the season. A loss to Seattle, a win over Tampa Bay, a big, 24-3, loss to the lowly Giants. Steve was just nine of 24 for 94 yards as he hurt a hip which would cause him to miss two games and bother him the rest of the year. He had a good day in a win over San Diego, hitting 17 of 30 for 225 yards and three scores, but by then it was too late. The club split its final two games and finished the year a very disappointing 6-10.

Steve's stats for 1979 showed a lot of personal highs. He completed 203 of 379 passes for 2,502 yards, a passing percentage of 53.6, 17 touchdowns, and 20 intercepts. But even Steve himself was not satisfied with his season and was the first to admit it.

"I know I was an inconsistent quarterback all year," he said. "There were some bad interceptions and a lot of things I could have done differently. I also had some minor physical problems that added up and might have affected my performance. I hurt a finger on my throwing hand in the preseason and it never did heal right and the hip injury against the Giants bothered me the rest of the season. Sometimes you can only play as well as you feel. But there were also times when I just plain forced the ball. There's simply no excuse to that."

Then in early February of 1980, there could have been a real setback. Steve was playing basketball and was bringing the ball upcourt when he suddenly felt pain in his surgically repaired right knee. An examination revealed another cartilage tear. But this time he didn't need major surgery. He had arthroscope surgery performed. That's when the surgeons go in through small holes in the knee and clean out the damaged areas. Since they don't actually cut the knee, recovery is swift.

In Steve's case, they not only cleaned up the new tear,

but spotted a couple of old ones as well. The whole thing might have been a blessing in disguise because Steve said that during the Tampa Bay game in 1979 he thought the knee almost dislocated while he was running the ball out of bounds.

"From what the doctors are saying, those old injuries could have been causing all kinds of problems," he revealed. "Now they think it's going to be better than it was."

It was also hoped the Falcons would be better. The team felt it had an outstanding draft. They picked up tight end Junior Miller from Nebraska, a 6-4, 235-pounder with outstanding speed. It was hoped he could replace the departed Jim Mitchell and also give Steve another deep threat. In addition, they picked up two fast, aggressive linebackers, Buddy Curry and Al Richardson, who would fit into the swarming, 3-4, defense the team was now using. They hoped for continued improvement from second-year runners Andrews (who gained 1,023 yards as a rookie) and Cain (coming off knee surgery) and more consistency from Steve Bartkowski. They also wanted the NFC Western title and a trip to the Super Bowl. Not much to ask.

By the preseason, Steve was very optimistic. His knee felt stronger than it had since he first hurt it. His rededication to God had really stabilized his personal life, and he had also remarried and was extremely happy. So he felt he was ready both mentally and physically to produce a big season.

It ended up in disappointment the first week. The club lost a close one to Minnesota, 24-23, the kind every team likes to win. Steve was just average with 14 of 28 for 165 yards and two scores. But the team found out that Lynn Cain had recovered from his knee injury as he gained 123 yards. They would find out very quick what the team was made of, because it was almost imperative they win their second game against a very good New England team.

They found out quickly. The first half was a donnybrook and the Falcons got the best of it. Steve hit on TD passes to Francis, the rookie Miller, and Miller again. Andrews scored on the ground and Atlanta had a 28-21 halftime lead. The defense took over the second half and pitched a shutout and the Falcons won it, 37-21.

Steve had a big day with 19 of 30 for 244 yards. Andrews rambled for 124 yards and rookie Miller had eight catches for 117 yards. Suddenly, the Falcon offense seemed balanced and awesome. Now if they could find consistency they would be a very, very tough team to beat.

Well, for three periods against Miami it looked as if they had. They took a 14-3 lead into the final session . . . and blew it. The Dolphins scored 17 points and won, 20-17. The ground attack slowed, but Steve had a very big day with 18 of 36 for 332 yards. Jenkins was the big catcher with four for 126 yards. The Falcons felt they had the gamebreakers and shouldn't have let this one get away. After three games, however, Steve was the second leading passer in the AFC behind Ron Jaworski of Philadelphia.

There were mixed reviews the following week. Top billing went to the victory. The Falcons beat the 49ers, 20-17, with Andrews gaining 100 yards. On the negative side was the 345 yards 49er quarterback Steve DeBerg was able to rack up, as well as the paltry 90 yards that Bartkowski could manage. Steve just couldn't get it going, but he compensated by not making mistakes and directing the team flawlessly in other ways. The club was now 2-2 and knocked the 49ers from the ranks of the unbeaten.

The next game belonged to the defense. Facing the

Detroit Lions, the Falcons swept to a 34-6 halftime lead and went on to take a 43-28 victory. Rookie linebacker Buddy Curry ran back a fumble 30 yards for a score, and linebacker Joel Williams took one back 42 yards. There was also a safety and a 42-yard Bartkowski to Jenkins TD toss in the early barrage. Steve was 11 for 22 for 183 yards.

The Falcons, Rams, and 49ers were all tied for the division lead with 3-2 records, though most people figured the perennial champs, the Rams, would begin pulling away. That's how it looked the next week when L.A. beat the Cardinals and the Falcons found themselves upset by the New York Jets, a team that had lost its first five games. Going in, the Falcon defense against the run was best in the league, but the Jets unleased a fine ground attack and won, 14-7. Steve fumbled a snap in the final period and the Jets recovered, leading to the winning score.

It was an embarrassing defeat. Steve was 20 of 31, but for only 168 yards. He couldn't go deep. It was also obvious that the Falcons couldn't keep up this roller-coaster play, win one, lose one. They had to go on a tear and stop playing flat against the poorer teams. Otherwise they were headed back for the scrap heap.

They rebounded again, but it was against the winless Saints and not much of a test. Winning it 41-14, Steve threw for four scores, two of them to rookie Miller. Then came the big one against the Rams, with Steve squaring off against his former college teammate, Vince Ferragamo. It was a rugged defensive battle for three periods, and going into the fourth the Rams held a 10-6 lead, a missed extra point hurting Atlanta. The whole season might be riding on the outcome of this game.

The L.A. defense held for most of the session. Then with just 2:22 left, the Falcons got the ball at their own 33 and started a final drive. Steve was sacked hard once, then made a first down. But the L.A. defenders poured in, sacking him twice more and leaving the Falcons with a third and 38 from their own 19. It looked about over.

But Steve stayed cool. He kept his backs in to block and rifled a bullet to Alfred Jackson at the Atlanta 46. That made it fourth and 11. But instead of just passing for the first down, Steve surprised the Rams, finding Jackson isolated on Pat Thomas, and he hit his wide receiver for a 54-yard touchdown play, perhaps the biggest throw of Steve's career. The kick gave the Falcons a 13-10 victory and put them back in the division race.

"What it amounted to was two prayer passes," Steve said with a wink, "and I never had an aversion to prayer."

The L.A. game seemed to light a fire under the Falcons. Beating a very good Buffalo team, 30-14, with a balanced attack, they took the Cardinals, 33-27, as Steve had the biggest day of his career. He hit on 31 of 47 passes for a whopping 378 yards and he did it the hard way since the Cards led at halftime, 24-6.

"I think St. Louis forgot about us, that we had any chance to win," Steve said. "It may sound like I'm tooting my own horn, but I like being behind because it gives me the opportunity to do what I like best, and that's throw the football."

Steve's newfound confidence was contagious. He now felt he could throw against any defense in the league, and the Falcons were beginning to believe they could beat anyone. They had a one-game lead on the Rams with a 7-3 record and wanted to stay there.

They continued to roll, whipping New Orleans again, 31-13, as Steve threw for three scores and received some high praise from his coach.

"Bart is definitely one of the reasons we are where we are," Leeman Bennett said. "He got knocked down a couple of times, but he came back and hung in there. In the past, he has not always done that."

Then the win streak reached six with a 28-17 victory over Chicago. Steve was 17 for 32 for 250 yards, with three more scores. Next, the Redskins fell, 10-6, Andrews getting 111 yards and going over 1,000 for the second straight year. Then in a game against the 11-2 Eagles, they won again, 20-17, Steve firing for two more scores and Andrews getting 101 yards. The club was 11-3, tied with Philly and Dallas for the best record in the league. Now with two games left, they were close to a division title.

A 35-10 victory over the 49ers did it, making the club 12-3, and winners of nine straight. The streak was broken by the Rams in the finale, 20-17, but a letdown was in order. After all, the club had just completed the greatest season in its history and tied for the best record in the league. Plus they were in the playoffs and didn't have to go through a wildcard game.

And what a season it had been, especially for Steve Bartkowski. He hit on 257 of 463 passes for 3,544 yards, and a 55.5 percentage. His 31 touchdowns passes was the best in the entire league, and he threw just 16 interceptions. He was the third-rated quarterback in the NFC, fourth highest in the league. And to many, he was the most explosive of them all in 1980.

He wasn't the only one. Andrews finished with 1,308 yards and a 4.9 average per carry, third best in the NFC. Lynn Cain gained 914 yards, also having a great year. Alfred Jenkins was the club's top receiver with 57 catches for 1,026 yards and six scores. Wallace Francis had 54 catches for 862 yards, Andrews had 51 for 456, while rookie Miller had 46 for 574. The entire offensive unit played well, and the defense was tops. After 15 years in the NFL, the Falcons were finally a powerful, balanced, and deep team. It was felt they had as good a chance as anyone to win it all.

The Falcons first playoff opponent would be the Dallas Cowboys, the team that had eliminated them in 1978, and the game promised to be a tough one. In the first quarter, however, the Falcons made it look easy for their hometown fans. Mazzetti opened the scoring with a 28-yard field goal. Then, before the period ended, Steve went to work. From his own 40, he threw deep to Alfred Jenkins, and hit the fleet receiver with a perfect strike for a 60-yard touchdown. The kick made it 10-0.

Dallas got a field goal at the end of the period, then tied it in the second on a short pass from Danny White to Billy Joe Dupree. But a Lynn Cain run put the Falcons up 17-10 at the half.

In the third period, it was beginning to look as if the Falcons would ice it. Midway through the period Steve got his club started on their 30, and in six plays he marched them 70 yards for another score. Andrews had runs of nine and 12 yards, and Steve hit Jenkins on a key, 22-yard pass. The score came on another pass, 12 yards from Steve to Andrews. Mazzetti's kick made it 24-10, and that was still the score when the final session began.

But early in the period the Cowboys got one back, cutting it to 24-17. Mazzetti then kicked a 34-yard field goal following an interception by Tom Pridemore, making it 27-17, with less than seven minutes left. If the Falcons could hold, they'd be playing for the NFC championship.

The only problem was that Dallas refused to quit. With less than four minutes left they culminated a 62-yard drive in five plays, Drew Pearson catching three Danny White passes, the last for a 14-yard touchdown on a nifty grab between two defenders. It was now 27-24 with time winding down. A long drive would run out the

clock. But on a third down play after the kickoff, Dallas'
Too Tall Jones stopped Cain and the Falcons had to
punt.

Dallas now had the ball on its own 30 with 1:48 left.
White took to the air again, completing passes to Butch
Johnson, Preston Pearson, and Tony Dorsett, bring the
ball to the Atlanta 23 with a first down. The Falcons
decided to blitz, hoping to sack White and get the Cowboys out of field goal range. But the cagey White picked
it up and lofted a quick pass toward the end zone. Once
again Drew Pearson was there, gathering it in for the
winning touchdown with just 42 seconds left. The final
was 30-27, a heartbreaking defeat.

There was no way to explain it, no excuses. The
Falcons had played very well and were just nipped by a
veteran team with years of playoff experience under
their belts. The Falcon players were down, but they
could be proud. As Wallace Francis put it:

"That was the Super Bowl. The fans will not see another game better than this one this year."

And no one could fault Steve Bartkowski. Like the
rest of the Falcons he played very well. Steve completed
18 of 33 passes for 320 big yards and two scores. He had
the 60-yard TD strike to Jenkins and another 50-yarder
to the same man to set up another score. And like the
rest of the Falcons, Steve feels the team will be back.

"I think we've come of age now as a team and the
whole league knows it," Steve said. "No one is going to
look forward to playing us now."

That's true, and not many defensive units are going to
look forward to facing the rifle arm of Steve
Bartkowski. His is a story of success at several levels. He
saw it come, had it taken away, and then worked to re-
gain it, giving his life a whole new direction at the same
time.

"I just believe the Lord has given me a tremendous

peace about living and where I am and what I'm doing," he said, late in 1980. "I think He has me here with the Atlanta Falcons for a reason . . . I wasn't created to do the things I was doing before I met Him. Now, I'm on the track of life God wants me to be on."

And he's throwing touchdown passes to boot.

SIGNALCALLERS — PRO STATISTICS

Brian Sipe

Team	Year	Att.	Comp.	Pct.	Yards	TD	Int.	Ave. Gain
Cleveland	1972	TAXI SQUAD						
Cleveland	1973	TAXI SQUAD						
Cleveland	1974	108	59	54.6	603	1	7	5.6
Cleveland	1975	88	45	51.1	427	1	3	4.9
Cleveland	1976	312	178	57.1	2,113	17	14	6.8
Cleveland	1977	195	112	57.4	1,233	9	14	6.3
Cleveland	1978	399	222	55.6	2,906	21	15	7.3
Cleveland	1979	535	286	53.5	3,793	28	26	7.1
Cleveland	1980	554	337	60.8	4,132	30	14	7.5
Pro Totals		2,191	1,239	56.5	15,207	107	93	6.9

Joe Ferguson

Team	Year	Att.	Comp.	Pct.	Yards	TD	Int.	Ave. Gain
Buffalo	1973	164	73	44.5	939	4	10	5.7
Buffalo	1974	232	119	51.3	1,588	12	12	6.8
Buffalo	1975	321	169	52.6	2,426	25	17	7.5
Buffalo	1976	151	74	49.0	1,086	9	1	7.2
Buffalo	1977	457	221	48.4	2,803	12	24	6.1
Buffalo	1978	330	175	53.0	2,136	16	15	6.5
Buffalo	1979	458	238	52.0	3,572	14	15	7.8
Buffalo	1980	439	251	57.2	2,805	20	18	6.4
Pro Totals		2,552	1,320	51.7	17,355	112	112	6.8